INTERNATIONAL GRAPHIC DESIGN, ART & ILLUSTRATION

Editor: YUSAKU KAMEKURA

Publisher: RECRUIT CO., LTD.
Production: RECRUIT CREATIVE CENTER

Printing: TOPPAN PRINTING CO., LTD.
Distributors: RIKUYO-SHA PUBLISHING, INC.
WILLIAM E. YAMAGUCHI ASSOCIATES INC.
RECRUIT EUROPE LTD.

編集長 ——————— 亀倉雄策

編集アシスタント ——— 菊池雅美
　　　　　　　　　　　小関妙子

アートディレクター ——— 亀倉雄策

デザイナー ——————— 水上　寛
アシスタントデザイナー —— 加藤正巳
　　　　　　　　　　　廣田由紀子
プリンティングディレクター —— 小嶋茂子
英訳 ———————————— ロバート・ミンツァー

発行 ——————————— 1991年9月1日
定価 ——————————— 3,200円 (本体3,107円)
発行所 —————————— 株式会社 リクルート
　　　　　　　　　　　〒104 東京都中央区銀座8-4-17
　　　　　　　　　　　TEL.03-3575-7074 (編集室)
発行人 —————————— 位田尚隆
制作 ——————————— リクルートクリエイティブセンター
印刷 ——————————— 凸版印刷株式会社
用紙 ——————————— 特漉NKダルアート　日本加工製紙株式会社
発売 ——————————— 株式会社六耀社
　　　　　　　　　　　〒160 東京都新宿区新宿2-19-12 静岡銀行ビル
　　　　　　　　　　　TEL.03-3354-4020 FAX.03-3352-3106

世界のグラフィックデザイン, アート & イラストレーション

クリエイション

編集——亀倉雄策

発行——株式会社リクルート
制作——リクルートクリエイティブセンター

印刷——凸版印刷株式会社
発売——株式会社六耀社

Editor ——————— Yusaku Kamekura

Editorial assistants —— Masami Kikuchi
Taeko Koseki

Art director ———————— Yusaku Kamekura

Designer ——————————— Yutaka Mizukami
Assistant designers —— Masami Kato
Yukiko Hirota
Printing director ———— Shigeko Kojima
Translator ——————————— Robert A. Mintzer

CREATION No.10 1991
Publisher ——————————— Recruit Co., Ltd.
8-4-17 Ginza, Chuo-ku, Tokyo 104, Japan
TEL. 03-3575-7074 FAX. 03-3575-7077 (Editor's Office)
Production —————————— Recruit Creative Center
Printing ———————————— Toppan Printing Co., Ltd.
Distributors ————————— Rikuyo-sha Publishing, Inc.
Shizuoka Bank Bldg., 2-19-12 Shinjuku, Shinjuku-ku, Tokyo 160, Japan
TEL. 03-3354-4020 FAX. 03-3352-3106

William E. Yamaguchi Associates Inc.
225 East 57th Street, New York, N.Y. 10022 USA
TEL. 212-753-1224 FAX. 212-753-1255

Recruit Europe Ltd.
2/3 Bedford Street, London, U.K., WC2E 9HD
TEL. 071-497-8800 FAX. 071-836-0999

CONTENTS──目次

MILTON GLASER　　　　　　　James McMullan　　　　　　　　**8**
ミルトン・グレーサー　　　　　　　ジェームズ・マクマラン

ROBERTO RAMPINELLI　　　　Shunsuke Kijima　　　　　　　　**54**
ロベルト・ランピネーリ　　　　　　木島俊介

DUGALD STERMER　　　　　　Steven Heller　　　　　　　　　**70**
ドゥガルド・スターマー　　　　　　スティーブン・ヘラー

SHIN MATSUNAGA　　　　　　Mamoru Yonekura　　　　　　　**92**
松永 真　　　　　　　　　　　　　米倉 守

WIKTOR SADOWSKI　　　　　Noboru Matsuura　　　　　　　**112**
ヴィクトル・サドフスキ　　　　　　松浦 昇

HARUO TAKINO　　　　　　　Ikko Tanaka　　　　　　　　　**132**
滝野晴夫　　　　　　　　　　　　田中一光

ARTISTS' PROFILES　　　　　　　　　　　　　　　　　　**166**
作家略歴

Cover: MILTON GLASER

表紙：ミルトン・グレーサー

PREFACE TO No.10 10号のまえがき

Yusaku Kamekura 亀倉雄策

With this issue, *CREATION* has now reached the halfway mark in its slated production run of 20 volumes. Trite though it may sound, the past two and a half years have at times seemed quite short, at others quite long. In pondering my efforts at magazine editing in retrospect, I am struck by a complexity of thoughts. With the completion of each issue I have asked myself repeatedly if the results have been satisfactory. This is not to suggest that I have no confidence in my editing skills: I do. Yet to be truly honest, when I ask myself if I have done a "perfect" job, my response is inevitably "No."

As editor "omniponent," I have been able to apply my views unchallenged to my editorial policy. I confer with no one, and instinctively I accept the opinions of others only when they coincide with my own judgments. I rely not on theory or logic, but only on my intuitive sense. I perform my editorial work in my head, or scribbled on tiny scraps of paper. Such remarks might give the impression that I work haphazardly. Not so. In my mind's eye I continuously retain a clear visual image of forthcoming issues, much like projecting photographic slides on a screen.

In each issue I bring together unique artists from around the world and fit them like pieces of a puzzle. As interlocking parts of this puzzle, each generates a mutually enhancing energy resulting in a high level of tension that, if I succeed, runs straight through the volume from first page to last. Artists are selected based on three points: individual uniqueness, expressive power and quality. It matters not whether they are young or old, famous or unknown. I do, however, try to avoid choosing only those artists who fall in line with my personal tastes. I always attempt to be fair and unbiased in my selections.

As you have seen, *CREATION* contains very little written text. This is because my goal is to include as many graphic plates as possible, as large as possible. It suffices, I believe, for the accompanying text to provide a general overview of the artist and his work. The graphics, if laid out effectively, will convey his unique artistry more eloquently. Their effect is even greater when the pages give the reader a notion of the artist's human side. Here my aim is for the reader to acquire an understanding not through explanatory text, but through his own perceptions.

One reader, an instructor at an American design school, commented that he would like to see *CREATION* provide detailed explanations of each work featured. Without such annotations, he criticized, the magazine is inadequate as an educational tool. No doubt I would probably register the same complaint myself if I were an educator. As editor, however, I must reply that it is by no means my intention to produce *CREATION* as a textbook. I might add, though, that artists whose works are so lacking in expressive strength or the capacity to convey ideas without notes of explanation are, I should hope, not included in *CREATION* in the first place. Artists whose works have value comprehensible only through explanations are not worthy of inclusion in the magazine.

Creationも遂に10号という峠にさしかかった。全巻20号で終了ということだから、丁度半分ということである。平凡な感想だが、長いようで短い2年6か月だった。10号という道程を振り返って編集というものを考えると、いろいろ複雑な思いが、私の胸のなかを去来する。毎号、これでよかったかという自問自答をくり返してきた。それでは編集に対する自信がなかったのかと問われれば、「自信はあった」と答えられる。では、完璧だったかと問われれば「否」と答えるしかない。

責任編集というのは、私ひとりの思想が、そのまま編集方法に作用してゆく。私は誰かに相談することもなく、他人からの意見も、自分で判断して取り上げる性質のもの以外は、本能的に受け入れない。理論ではなく感性だけの直感である。だから編集は常に私の頭脳のなかか、ほんの小さな紙切れに書いたメモにしかない。では、場あたりの思いつきかと想像されるだろうが、そうではなく、いつも何号か先までのイメージは、スライドを映写するように、はっきりと私の瞼に浮かんでいる。いろいろな個性や表現を持った世界中の芸術家をパズルのように組み合わせる。極端な言い方をすると夜も昼も、そのパズルは私の頭のなかから消えることはない。パズルの組み合わせ方によって、優れた芸術家たちが発するエネルギーの相乗効果で1冊の本が出来上がる。だから最初の頁から最後の頁まで張りつめた緊張感が貫き通る筈だ。それだけに私自身、編集構成の総仕上げの段階に入るころ、夜中にふと目を覚ますと1頁、1頁のレイアウトの弱点が気になる。さらに掲載作家の力量が正しく誌面に表現されているかを考えると目が冴えてしまう。私はCreationに登場願う芸術家を個性、表現、質の3点に注目して選択している。古い新しい、有名無名は問題にしない。しかし自分の好みによる偏った表現の人だけの選択は避けている。常に平衡感覚に注意しなければならない。

Creationはごらんのように、きわめて文章が少ない。なるべく、多量の図版をたっぷりとしたサイズで展開しようとするからである。文章は掲載した芸術家の概念を伝達すれば充分だと私は考える。図版は効果的に配置することで、読者に作家の個性、芸術性を具体的に伝達する。さらに、その芸術家の人間性まで感じ取ってもらえれば、私の目的は成功したことになろう。解説的な文章の助けを借りて作家の人間性を感じ取るのではなく、自分の目で見て、自分の感性で感じ取ってほしいのだ。だから文章は概念であって説明ではないのだ。あるアメリカのデザイン学校の先生から「Creationの作品ひとつひとつにくわしい解説がほしい。これでは資料が足らず教育に適さない」というご注意をいただいた。恐らく私も教育者だったら同じ文句を言うだろう。しかし私はCreationを教科書にするつもりは毛頭ないのだ。解説がなければ理解されないような、表現力も伝達性も乏しい作家の作品はCreationには登場させないし、また解説を読まなければ、その作品の価値が理解されない人には、恐らくCreationは無縁な存在であろう。デザインの方法、技法といった、作り方を求める人には、このCreationは全く無力である。また注文されたデザインのヒントになる参考書としてもCreationは適さない。

CREATION admittedly serves no purpose for those who might seek to use it as a tool to learn about design techniques. Nor is the magazine appropriate as a reference work to provide hints to budding designers. *CREATION* is in fact an "antisocial" magazine: it is not geared to providing public services in any way. For these reasons it is also not expected to sell in great quantities—a situation which inevitably means that it generates no financial profit. Robert Delpire, the French design producer and publisher of cultural works, has asked me how I manage to put out *CREATION*. He said that in his experience, when he tried to publish his own "ideal" magazine he ultimately had to throw in the towel after just six issues. He added that it would surely be impossible for me to publish *CREATION* without powerful backup support. And Monsieur Delpire is absolutely right.

Just after the first issue of *CREATION* appeared, I received a letter from the renowned American illustrator Seymour Chwast. "I know what a major undertaking it must be to create, produce, edit, and art direct any publication," he said. "But, being able to show to the world your personal view of what is important in graphic design must give you great satisfaction." At the time, I was still unable to understand what this "great satisfaction" might be. But as I proceeded through the second issue, and then the third, I began to sense this satisfaction like a refreshing breeze blowing through my soul. Seymour Chwast, I came to realize, is a man who knows much about life. He was able to peer into the future and see where my work would lead me.

Today I recognize that I am constantly striving to produce work that will provide me with a sense of satisfaction, which I now know is one of the greatest joys in the solitary realm of editing. Unfortunately, satisfaction equates with a determination never to compromise one's editorial principles in any way, and this is a determination that cannot be carried through unless one is cold-hearted and unshackled by sympathy for others—traits certainly not worthy of pride. From this one must conclude that personal fulfillment is really nothing but the complacency of a perfectionist—and most perfectionists are stubborn and self-righteous. The joy of personal satisfaction is thus something acquired at a heavy price.

With 10 issues completed and another 10 remaining, the next two and a half years will continue to be a steep climb. I cannot deny that this precipitous path will be tread with certain anxieties along the way. For the more one comes to know about editing, the more he learns just how difficult and frightening it is. Readers may perhaps come to feel that the magazine has gotten in a rut. Even I may come to harbor doubts about the wisdom of pursuing the present style unaltered. Maybe I will wander from the trail, shedding my confidence en route, being forced to confront the weakness and fragility of man. Should I lose the battle, my satisfaction will fade to a memory.

When I close my eyes, on my mental·screen I see a slide of myself walking in solitude against a bleak and desolate background.

Creationにはそういうサービス精神がまるでない、無愛想な本である。無愛想な本だから多量に売れるというものではない。限られた部数の出版だから当然利益は生れない。はからずもフランスのデザインプロデューサーであり、文化的な出版者でもあるロベルト・デルピールが私に「カメクラ、一体どういう方法でCreationを出しているんだ。自分の経験なんだが、私が理想とする雑誌を出版したものの、6号で遂にお手上げになった。Creationのような本は強力な後押しがなければ実現出来ないんだよ」と言った。さすがにご明察である。

Creationが創刊された時、アメリカの高名なイラストレーターのシーモア・クワストから「どんな出版物も制作する、プロデュースする、編集する、アートデレクションすることはとても大変な仕事だが、世界に向けてグラフィックデザインの何が重要かを自分の視点で表現できるのだから、きっと充実感を味わうことだろう」という手紙をいただいた。まだ、この手紙の時点では、その充実感という意味がよく理解出来なかった。そうして2号から3号と進むうちに、シーモア・クワストがいう充実感が爽やかに胸の中を吹き抜けるように思われてきた。彼は、やっぱり人生の達人だったのだ。彼は私の仕事の先を見透かしていたのだ。たしかに今、この充実感を獲得するために出来るだけ力を絞りだそうとする自分の姿勢を感じることが出来る。編集という孤独な作業のなかでの大きな喜びは充実感である。実は、充実感とは1点の妥協も許さないという決意にほかならないのだ。この決意というのは、人情にほだされない冷徹な心でないと実行出来ない。しかし冷徹な心なんて、全く嫌なものだと思う。結論から申し上げると、充実感というのは完全主義者の自己満足なんだ。完全主義者のほとんどは頑固で独善的なんだ。だから充実感のよろこびというのは大変な代償を払っているということだろうか。

10号の峠を越えて、さらに11号、12号と20号の終結までの2年6か月は急な山道を登り続けることになる。その急坂に不安はないかと問われれば、それは「当然ある」と答えるしかない。それは編集というものがわかってくればくるほど編集のむずかしさ、恐ろしさを感じるものだからだ。そして読者からマンネリズムだと指摘されるかも知れないし、私自身、このままのスタイルでいいのかという疑問も起きてくる。したがって迷いも起きるし自信も失ってしまう。そうして人間のもろさ、弱さと戦うことになる。この戦いに敗れれば、充実感など夢物語になってしまう。いささかセンチメンタルな表現だが、じっと瞼を閉じれば、荒涼とした風景のなかを孤独に歩き続ける自分の姿がスライドを見るように見えてくるのだ。

MILTON GLASER ミルトン・グレーサー

James McMullan ジェームズ・マクマラン

The secret of Milton Glaser's work is in his lunch conversation. He has, at lunch with me, explained the link between Hopi gift rituals and the prices in Soho galleries and then seamlessly switched the topic to revealing how duck liver contributes to the flavor of the black beans we are eating. The scope of his conversation not only marks him as an educated, hungry man, but also hints at the underlying contrary forces at work in his art.

I have always imagined Milton with two muses hovering over his head as he works; one is a restless, skinny theoretician, tapping him every once in a while with a ruler, and the other is a robust chef, showering him from time to time with dark, ripe cherries. The outcome, as we know, is that Milton takes the cherries and the ruler and bakes a delicious pie that also happens to conform to the proportions of the Golden Mean.

The fact that Milton, responding to challenges as different as book jackets and supermarkets, creates terrific cherry pies time after time, does not lessen the drama of the synthesis he achieves. His theorist and his chef represent many different impulses tugging him in opposite directions. He is attracted, for instance, to the formality of artists such as Piero della Francesca while, at the same time, he loves the zany undulations of Mickey Mouse. He often plays with grids and circles, but only so he can pop open their geometry with insistent natural forms. On the other hand he undermines the charming chaos of his landscapes with more than a hint of Euclidian order. He is drawn to architecture, particularly columns and arches, but deconstructs their solidity with lines and planes that slice and dice them back down to the flat surface. He has done hundreds of heads but disdains likeness. He loves magic but presents it to us in such a coolly revealing way that we end up on the magician's side of the mirrored box. He never tires of finding new ways of organizing Chinese vegetables or the moods of Mozart into grids, but his elegant puzzles never lead to anything as simple as good, better, best, or a conclusion about Mozart. He speaks wonderfully about the clarity we achieve by sticking to the shared language of visual clichés, and then he turns around and makes a success of the most personal and idiosyncratic image.

Milton, caught between his theoretician and his chef, is amazingly calm. I don't have the impression that he knows what he is going to do as he contemplates each problem, because his responses are so unstandardized, but he seems to gain energy and resolve from having to quickly find inspiration in the fluid territory between his extremes. Quickness, in fact, plays a large part in the way that Milton operates. There is an impatience in him with anything that must be arrived at in small increments over a long period of time, so he needs to keep moving in the way that he arrives at ideas and carries them out. It is as though his two muses would fall out of balance if he didn't keep them going at a solid gallop. One of the gentle ironies of his life is that he had the great, good fortune to study in Italy with Giorgio Morandi, an artist of exquisite patience, who, in both his slow careful approach to making an image and

ミルトン・グレーサーの作品の秘密はランチの会話の中にある。彼は私と昼食をとりながら、ホピ族の贈答儀礼とソーホーのギャラリーの値段の関係を説明し、その後ごく自然に鴨のレバーが今食べている黒豆の味にどのように影響しているかを話し始めるのである。その幅広い話題から、彼が単に教養ある貪欲な男であることだけでなく、仕事のベースに2つの対極する力があることがうかがえる。

私はいつも、ミルトンが仕事をする時、頭上に2人の神様がまとわりついているような気がした。ひとりは時々彼を定規でたたく落ち着きのない痩せこけた理論家。もうひとりは時折彼に色濃く熟したチェリーをふり注ぐ強固なシェフ。その結果ご存知のとおり、ミルトンはチェリーと定規を手においしいパイを焼き、それがまた黄金分割の法則による調和のとれたものなのである。

本のジャケットからスーパーマーケットに至るまで、ミルトンは毎回見事なチェリーパイを作るが、それは生易しいことではなく、彼の理論家とシェフとが劇的に作り上げるものなのである。理論家とシェフは、互いに彼を逆の方向に引きつける多くの衝撃を象徴する。例えば、彼は、ピエロ・デッラ・フランチェスカの様式美に魅せられる一方で、ミッキー・マウスの滑稽な動きも好む。時にグリッドや円を使うが、その幾何学的な中にいつも自然を取り入れる。逆に風景画の魅力的なアンバランスさの中に、ユークリッド幾何学的な秩序を取り入れる。彼は円柱やアーチなどの建築物に引かれているが、その立体を線や平面で分解し、細かく切り刻んで平らな面にしてしまう。何百もの頭像を描くが、単なる写実は決して好まない。マジックを愛するが、我々をミラーボックスのマジシャン側に立たせて冷ややかに見せる。彼は中国野菜やモーツァルトの雰囲気をグリッドの中に構成する、新しい手法の発見には貪欲だが、その優雅なパズルは中国野菜やモーツァルトについての結論を導くことはない。彼はありきたりのビジュアルという共通言語を通じて得られる明快さを熱心に語りながらも、逆に強烈な独自のイメージを作り出すことに成功している。

ミルトンは彼の理論家とシェフの間に立ちながら、驚くほど落ち着いている。彼は問題に立ち向かうたび、自分で何をすべきか分かっていないように見える。それは彼の答が普通とかけ離れているからだが、彼の両極の間で素早く発想しなければならないという状況からエネルギーが生まれ、問題解決をしているように思える。その素早さこそ、実は彼のやり方で重要な点である。彼は時間をかけて、じっくり取り組むのに我慢できない。だからアイディアを生み、実行するために常に動き回る必要があるのである。まるで2人の神々を全力疾走させないとバランスを失ってしまうようである。彼の人生でちょっとした皮肉といえるのは、幸運にもイタリアでジョルジョ・モランディという非常に忍耐強い芸術家の下に学んだということである。モランディはイメージを作るのに、じっくり構えてごく少ないアイディアをもとにする。ミルトンとは実に対照的だ。さらに皮肉なのはミルトンが他の誰よりもモランディに影響を受けていることである。クロスハッチ画法だけでなく、文学的アイディアや、作品から出る力強さも影響を受けている。

モランディに影響されている(特に1991年のイタリアでの展覧会で展示した

1 Illustration for record jacket レコードジャケットのイラストレーション 1975

2 Illustration for record jacket レコードジャケットのイラストレーション 1979

in how he based all his art on two or three ideas, represents a polar opposite to Milton. The further irony, of course, is that Milton has been more affected in his art by Morandi than by anyone else not only in the possibilities of crosshatch drawing but also in that particular power of a picture that comes from its emanations as much as from its literary idea.

Despite the influence of Morandi's life and art on Milton (particularly in the reflective quietness of his recent "Piero" drawings for the 1991 Italian exhibit), the dynamic of most of his work is a great deal larger and more overt than Morandi's. His theoretician and his chef are not making quiet electricity for him; they are usually making thunderbolts. When Milton invents an idea, it operates with dramatic simplicity and with an eloquence that can't be missed. Small is very small, big is huge, black is deepest night, light is clearest day, color is a Hindu rainbow, horror is a Victorian tabloid, death is Mexican in all its festival boniness, and life is an Italian-Jewish picnic.

This is a lot of muchness to bake into the pie of anyone's art—extreme bigness and smallness, blackness and whiteness (to say nothing of the theoretician always adding a dash of restraint to the gusto of the chef), but what eventually brings all these forces together successfully for Milton is the unerring grace of the work. Like a cat falling through the air, but always finding the horizon line and landing on its feet, Milton never seems to lose touch with the center of gravity in his own nervous system. Even in his most cerebral and stylized work, we feel the sureness of the way his hand creates shape and chooses interval. He stays connected, through all the twists and turns of his art, to the authentic personality of his drawing and the forms that it can invent for him. Reading these shapes at the most fundamental level we find a sensibility of extraordinary lyric power. The edges swoop and bulge with an effortless felicity, and yet dominate the space with a dense assertiveness. It is a curious mixture to find, this deftness and this anchoredness. On the one hand, we sense a natural impulse to harmonic curviness, and on the other, to an almost heavy stability in the way that the forms lock into their field. It is like having architecturally satisfying butterflies or even, as Milton has shown us, angels rooted to their aura. He uses one force, a classic stillness, to contrast, and paradoxically emphasize, a force of Baroque energy. When I think of the deepest response I have to his art, I am reminded of Matisse. What resonates for me is a lyricism which, like Matisse's, affirms the pleasure and balance of life, the civilization we can find through the harmony of art.

The tussle between the theorist and the chef in Milton's creative upper room is never quite resolved. It keeps the work hovering in a territory which is both cool and hot at the same time, luscious and contemplative, decorative and full of meaning, overflowing and stringent—a territory unlike anyone else's, a rather large, diverse country called Milton Glaser.

近作「ピエロ」のもの静かさに見られる）にもかかわらず、彼の作品の原動力はモランディを越えてさらに大きく、明らかである。理論家とシェフは、彼に弱い刺激を与えるのではなく、それどころかいつも強烈なパワーを与えているのである。ミルトンのアイディアは非常に単純で、また誰にでもすぐ分かる説得力がある。小さいものは非常に小さく、大きいものは巨大。黒は夜の闇のようで、光は晴れ渡った日のようである。色彩はヒンズー教の虹、恐怖はビクトリア調のタブロイド新聞、死はメキシコの陽気な祭、そして人生はイタリア系ユダヤ人のピクニックのようである。

ひとつのパイにこれだけのものをまとめるのは大変である。巨大さと極小さ、黒さと白さ（もちろん理論家はシェフの作る味に抑えを加える）、しかしこれらのものを全てうまくまとめあげるのは、あのなんとも言えない優雅さである。猫が宙を舞い落ちながらも平衡感覚を持って着地するように、ミルトンの神経は重心を見失うことはないようだ。彼が最も頭を使った様式化された作品にも、彼の手が形を作り、間を選ぶという確かさを感じることができる。彼は作品の全ての変革を通じて、作品の確かな独自性と、それが生み出す形を守っている。もっとも基本的な段階にあるそれの形から、非常に叙情的な力のある感性を見いだすことができる。それぞれの形の縁が下降したりふくらんだりするが、同時にどっしりした説得力をみなぎらせている。軽さと安定の奇妙な組み合わせだ。調和のとれた曲線へ、また同時に、固定された形の安定感への自然な衝動が感じられる。これは構造的に申し分のない蝶、もしくはミルトン自身が示すように、オーラに根ざした天使のようだ。彼は古典的な静寂というひとつの力を用いてバロック風の力に対比し、同時にそれを強調しているのである。彼の作品で最も深く感じることは、マチスのものと同じである。私の心に響くのはミルトンの作品の叙情主義だが、それはマチスのものと同様、人生の楽しさやバランス、芸術の調和に見られる文化文明を主張する。

ミルトンが理論家とシェフの間で揺れる葛藤は、いつまでも完全に解決されることなく残る。そしてこの葛藤が彼の作品を、冷たさと熱さ、甘美と静寂、装飾と意味、氾濫と逼迫、そういったものの間を絶えず漂わせている。そしてその間とは、他の誰のものとも異なりミルトン・グレーサーという大きく広い領域なのである。

Angel and landscape from the Nativity July 4th

3 "Angel and Landscape" 「天使と風景」 1990

4 "Landscape from the Nativity" 「キリスト降誕の風景」 1990

5 "Singing Angels"「歌う天使たち」1990

6 "Stranger in Piero's Landscape"「ピエーロの風景の見知らぬ人」1990

7 Poster for Olivetti オリベッティのポスター 1968

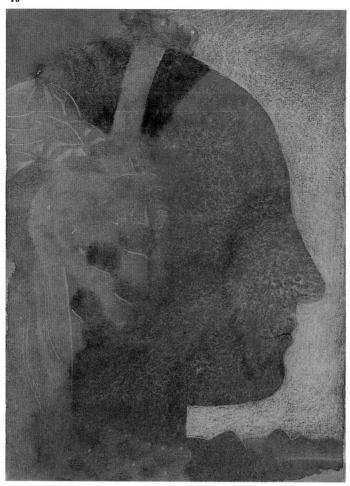

8 "Head of Battista in Blue" 「青いバティスタの頭」1990

9 "Head of Federico in Red" 「赤いフェデリコの頭」1990

10 "Roman Soldier from the Resurrection" 「キリスト復活におけるローマの戦士」1990

11 Poster for poster company ポスター会社のポスター 1977

12 Drawing of Apollinaire アポリネールの像 1960s

13 "Follies Girl" 「レビューガール」 1964

14 Magazine illustration 雑誌イラストレーション 1960s

15 "Nude" 「ヌード」 1970s

Of course one vote doesn't count.
Until you count all the people who think that way.

Barney's would like to remind you that polls in N.Y. will be open tomorrow 6 a.m. to 9 p.m.

16   Advertisement encouraging people to vote   投票促進のポスター   1975

17 Magazine illustration 雑誌イラストレーション 1960s

18　Illustration for Albert King poster　アルバート・キングのポスターのイラストレーション 1976

19 Illustration for Hermann Hesse calendar ヘルマン・ヘッセのカレンダーのイラストレーション 1974

20 Poster commemorating 100th anniversary of van Gogh's birth ヴァン・ゴッホ生誕100周年ポスター 1989

21 Poster for series of concerts コンサートシリーズのポスター 1973

22

23

22-24 Pages from Tuscany sketchbook トスカーナのスケッチブックより 1989

25　Illustration for book club poster　ブッククラブのポスターのイラストレーション　1986

26

27

26-28 "Mexican Skies"「メキシコの空」1983

29 "View Near Radda" 「ラッダ近辺の風景」1989

30 "View from Greve" 「グレヴェからの風景」1989

31 "View from Volpaia" 「ヴォルパイアからの風景」 1989

32 "Claude Monet"「クロード・モネ」1981

MONET

1840-1926　　　　　　　　　GIVERNY

33 Poster of Monet　モネのポスター　1982

Klimt war eine der einflußreichsten Persönlichkeiten der Wiener
Sezession. Die von ihm bevorzugte Ornamentik von Pflanzen-
formen und Figuren sind Grundlage dieses Blattes.

Klimt was one of the most influential figures in the Viennese
secessionist movement. Ornaments of plant forms and figures
preferred by the painter are the basis for this page.

Klimt fut l'une des personnalités les plus influentes de la
Sécession viennoise. Les ornements qu'il préférait – des formes
végétales et des figures – constituent la base de cette feuille.

(1862–1918)
GUSTAV KLIMT

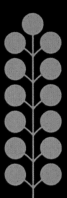

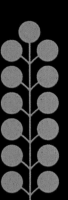

36　"Max Ernst"「マックス・エルンスト」1984

35　"Edvard Munch"「エドヴァルド・ムンク」1984

37　"Giorgio de Chirico"「ジョルジオ・デ・キリコ」1984

38　"Georgia O'Keeffe"「ジョージア・オキーフ」1984

40　"Piet Mondrian"「ピエト・モンドリアン」1984

39　"Paul Klee"「パウル・クレー」1984

Sonia Delaunays Porträt reflektiert ihr charakteristisches Vokabular von Kreisformen und leuchtenden Farben. Als Vorlage diente eine Fotografie, die sie in einem Kostüm zeigt, das von ihr selbst entworfen wurde.

Delaunay's portrait reflects her characteristic vocabulary of circular forms and heightened colour. It's based on a photograph showing her in a costume of her own design.

Le portrait de Sonia Delaunay reflète son vocabulaire caractéristique de formes circulaires et de couleurs éclatantes. Il est basé sur une photographie qui la montre dans un costume qu'elle avait dessiné elle-même.

(1885–1979)
SONIA DELAUNAY

ZANDERS

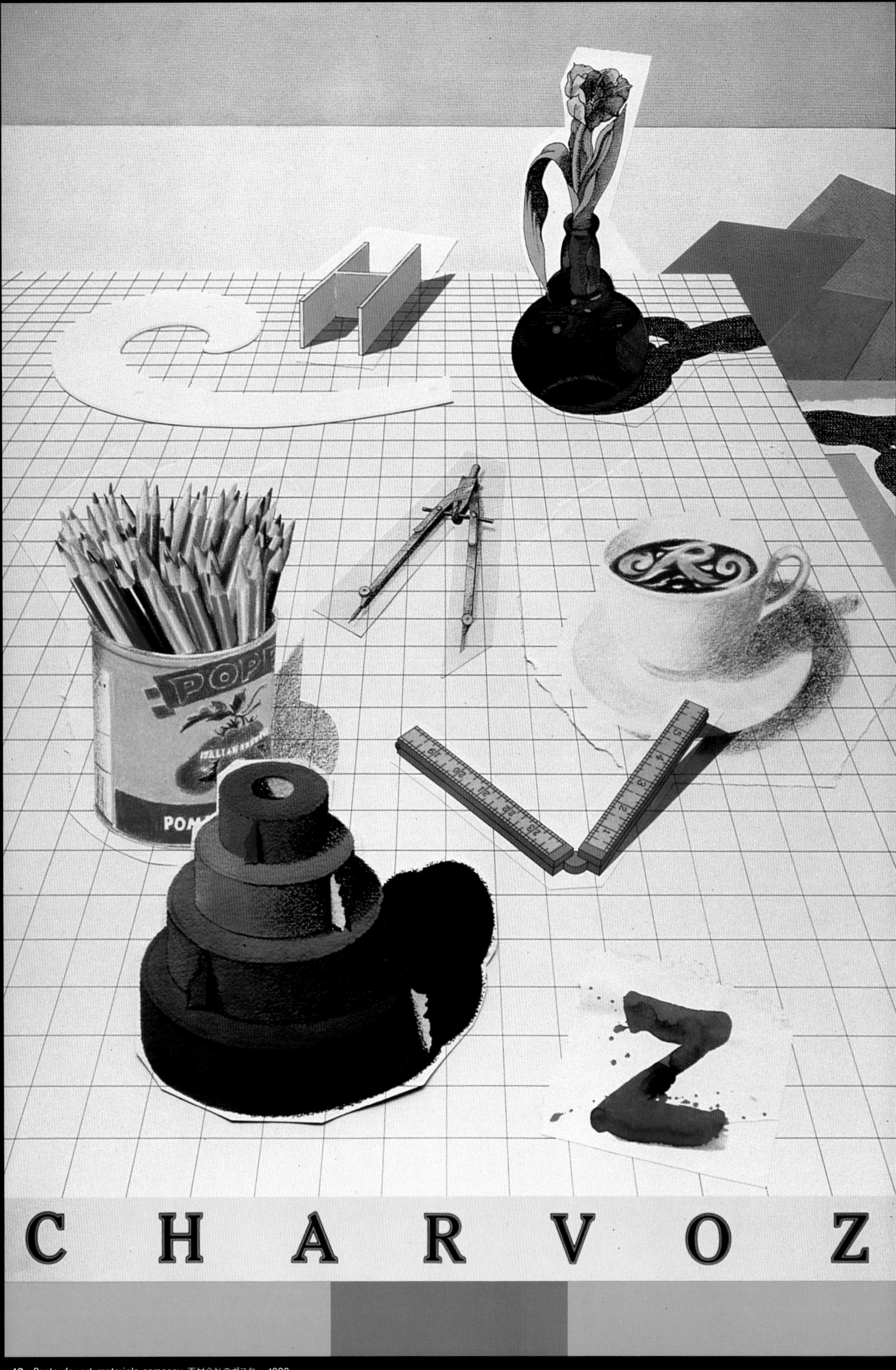

42 Poster for art materials company 画材会社のポスター 1986

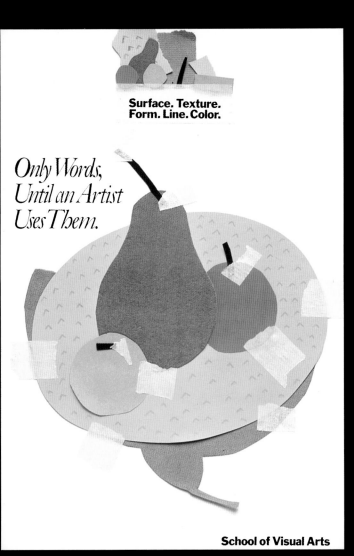

Surface. Texture.
Form. Line. Color.

Only Words,
Until an Artist
Uses Them.

School of Visual Arts

43   Poster for art school   美術学校のポスター 1985

Jubilee

Queens College
invites you to it's fiftieth
birthday celebration;
a year to rejoice, reflect,
reaffirm our devotion
to World-class education,
comparable to the
nation's elite colleges,
at a cost that towers
beneath them. Call
(718-520-7322) for
a calendar of
celebration events.

QUEENS COLLEGE, CUNY

44   Cover for college bulletin   大学広報誌の表紙 1987

Let knowledge grow

Queens College, CUNY · Undergraduate Bulletin · 1988-1989

46　Poster for association of homes for aging　老人ホーム協会のポスター　1986

48　Poster promoting music tape　ミュージックテープのポスター　1980

JUILLIARD

This poster made possible by a grant from ⊕TDK.

49 Poster for music school 音楽学校のポスター 1987

50 Illustration for record jacket レコードジャケットのイラストレーション 1976

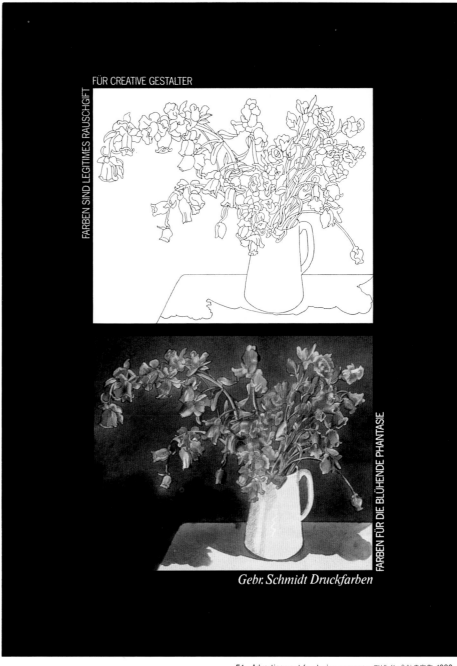

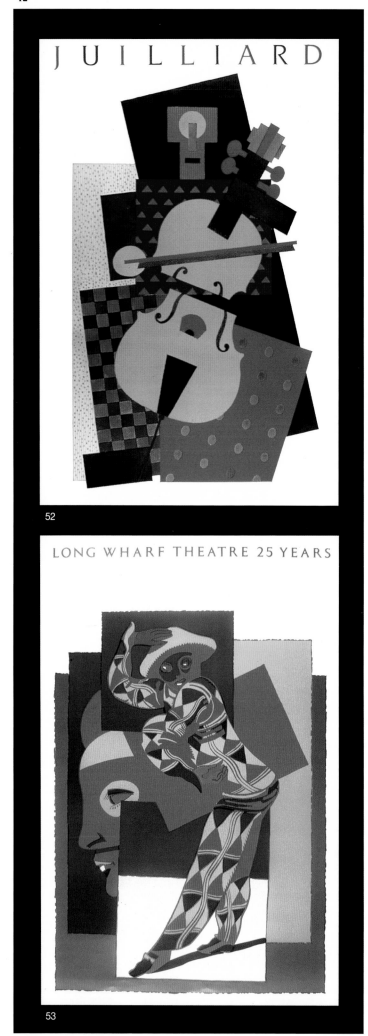

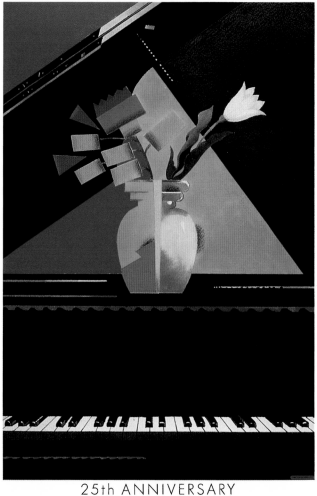

54 Poster for performing arts center 舞台芸術センターのポスター 1990

52 Poster for music school 音楽学校のポスター 1990   53 Theater poster 劇場のポスター 1989

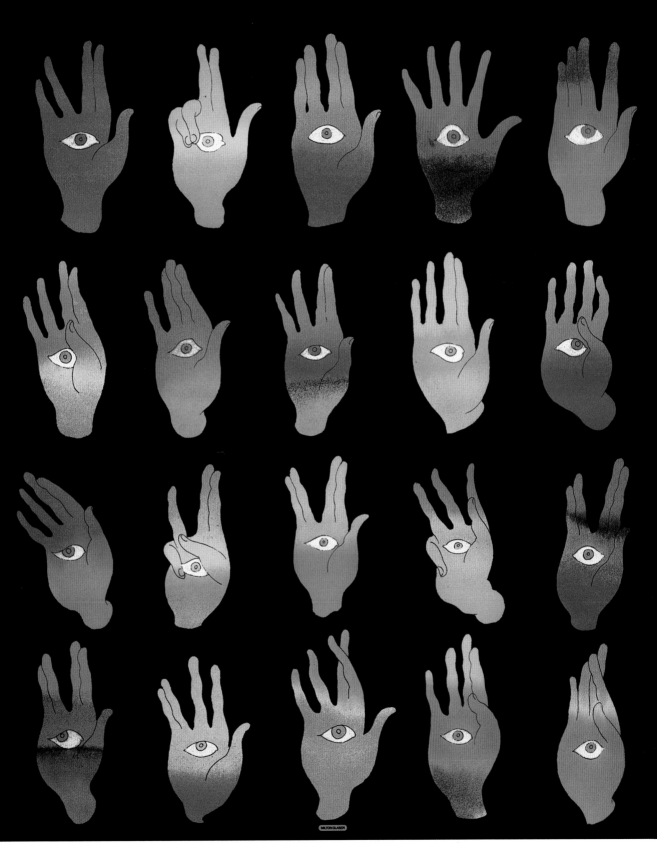

RIZZOLI GALLERIES: 712 FIFTH AVENUE, NEW YORK, OCTOBER 5, 1982
835 NORTH MICHIGAN AVENUE, CHICAGO, NOVEMBER 12, 1982

Great Illustrators of Our Time

VISIT A
MASTERPIECE

THE BROOKLYN MUSEUM
200 EASTERN PARKWAY / BROOKLYN, NEW YORK 11238

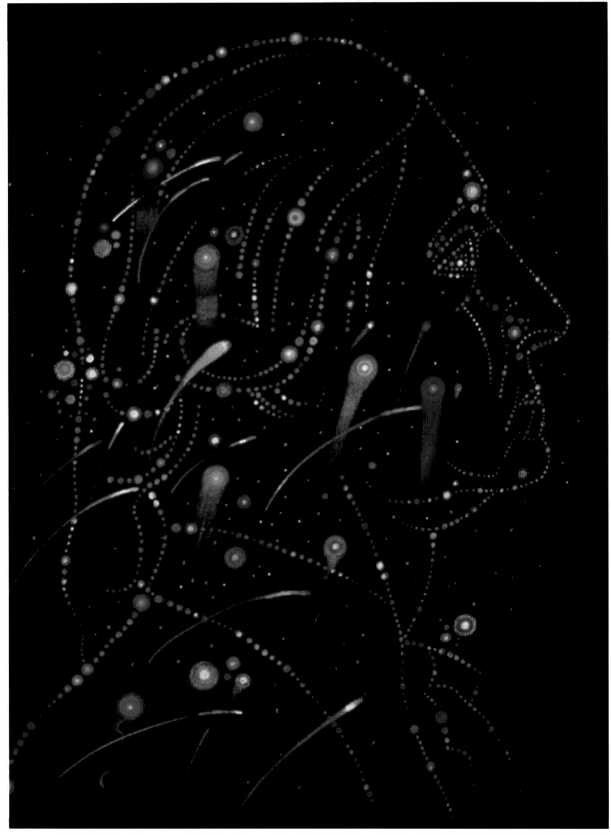

57 Illustration for poster commemorating 200th anniversary of George Washington's inauguration　ジョージ・ワシントン就任200周年ポスターのイラストレーション 1989

58 Poster for American Cello Congress アメリカチェロ大会のポスター 1986

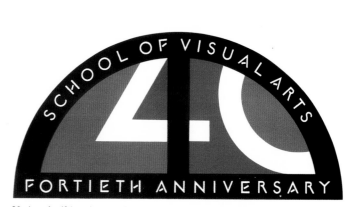

60 Logo for 40th anniversary of art school 美術学校40周年のロゴ 1987

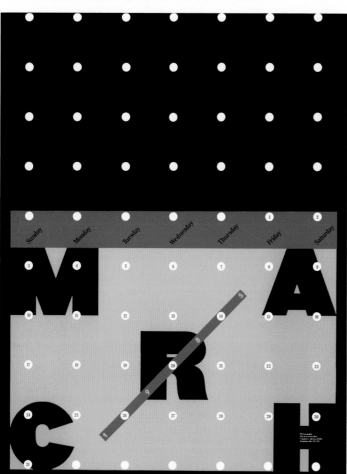

59 Calendar design カレンダーのデザイン 1985

61 Poster for 40th anniversary of art school 美術学校40周年のポスター 1987

64　Poster for Olivetti　オリベッティのポスター　1976

63　Poster for ink manufacturer　インクメーカーのポスター　1970s

65　Poster for Olivetti　オリベッティのポスター　1970s

67　Poster for art materials manufacturer　画材メーカーのポスター　1984

N E O

1 8

NEOCON 18

●

THE WORLD CONGRESS
ON ENVIRONMENTAL
PLANNING AND DESIGN

●

JUNE 10-13, 1986
THE MERCHANDISE MART
CHICAGO

C O N

69 Poster for congress on environmental planning and design 環境計画・デザイン会議のポスター 1986

ROBERTO RAMPINELLI ロベルト・ランピネーリ Painter

Shunsuke Kijima 木島俊介

The notion that painting is a technical ability to portray on canvas what one sees with his eyes originated, in my estimation, during the Renaissance in the 15th Century. Out of this conception there consequently developed a copious variety of techniques aimed at generating illusions of reality on canvas.

First, because real objects exist in three-dimensional realms, methods had to be devised to create illusions of three-dimensionality within the two-dimensional framework of a canvas. From this requirement emerged the two artistic methods of shading and highlighting. Additionally, to express the subtle and unique three-dimensional textural characteristics of individual substances, *sfumato* or gradation was developed. Next, since objects do not exist in physical isolation but rather occupy positions within ambient settings, scientific methods of perspective—linear perspective and aerial perspective—were conceived to express spatial relations. Finally, in the age of the Impressionists, a new method of coloring was invented whereby colors are applied to all objects in order to capture how they appear in light as seen by the human eye. With this, it seemed that the world had discovered the perfect method for reproducing Nature in art.

In what directions, however, has painting been moving in all the years thereafter? Indeed, where is it going today? In search of an answer to my eternal quest to know the "true meaning" of art, I have been powerfully attracted to the works of Roberto Rampinelli, an artist himself hailing from Italy, land of the Renaissance.

In Rampinelli's paintings, all objects exist in three dimensions. They possess colors all their own, and occupy positions in unified spatial realms perceived through use of light and shadow. The organic and the inorganic co-exist within these realms, clearly distinguishable from each other in their textural differences.

And yet, what is one to make of Rampinelli's withered flowers? To which category do they belong? Are they flora crumbling away in a setting of tranquil Nature? Are they organic objects metamorphosing to inorganic ones? I would suggest not.

Rampinelli is an expert at block printing. The phenomenally outstanding background description found in his oil paintings, treading a fine line between reality and unreality, perhaps derives from copperplate etchings which betray no traces of direct human intervention. It is this unique spatial realm of Rampinelli's, at the same time both organic and inoranic, both abstract and real, that has summoned up his withered flowers. Though once they possessed life, now they are lifeless. Though once they were organic, now they are inorganic. Though once they were objects of Nature, now they are material to be used by a painter. Have flower petals ever turned to minerals like this? Have rose branches ever withered to perfect squares? What are they if not the imaginary creations of the painter?

Contemporary artists know well that realism itself is but an illusion. In his works Rampinelli, while making a pretense of reality, is actually creating models of the painting style known as *natura morta*, "dead Nature," a human creation originally developed to induce melancholy.

絵画とは、自分の見ているものを描く技術であると考えられ始めたのは、15世紀、ルネッサンス時代のことであろうか。これより絵画は、画面上に現実のイリュージョンを生みだすための様々な技術を開発してきたのであった。現実の事物はまず立体として見えているから、画面という平面上に立体のイリュージョンを生み出す方法が創案されなければならない。こうして陰影法とハイライト法とが開発された。さらには物質が個々に備えている質感という、この微妙な立体感の表現のための、スフマート(ぼかし画法)の開発までもなされた。物はまた、それ自体で孤立してあるのではなく空間のなかに場を占めているのであるから、その空間をあらわすための科学的遠近法も考案された。線遠近法や空気遠近法である。加えて、印象派の時代となると、諸物に色を与えることで、それを人の眼に見せしめているところの光をとらえる新しい彩色法も発明されて、絵画はそれ自身のなかに、自然を再現させる完璧な方法を手に入れたかに思われたのであった。

さてそこから、絵画は何処へ行かんとしているのか。かのルネッサンスの地イタリアに生まれているランピネーリの仕事は、美術とはいったい何なのかと日々迷妄を重ねている私の関心を深くひきつけて止まないのだ。

ランピネーリの絵画では、個々の物は立体としてある。それらは固有の色を持ち、光と影とによって感じられる統一された空間の中に場を占めている。また無機物と有機物とが、明確な質感の区別を見せてそこに存在する。

ではいったい、この枯れた花は何なのか。この静謐な自然の中にあって倒壊しつつある植物か。無機物へと変容する有機物か。このリアリズムは自然の再現なのか。そうではあるまい。

ランピネーリは版画技術に精通している。彼の油絵に見られる現実とも非現実ともつかぬ秀逸な背景描写はおそらく、人の直接的な手業を感じさせない腐食銅版画のマチエールから来ているのだが、この有機的でもあり無機的でもある、抽象的でもあって具象的でもある独特の空間が、これらの枯れた花を呼び出してきたのだ。枯れた花は、かつては生命を持ち、今では生命を持たぬ存在、かつては有機物であったが、今では無機物となった存在、さらには、かつては自然物であったが、今では画家の手になる存在であることを暗示するものなのだ。これほどに鉱物と化した花弁があり、切り口が四角形に枯れてゆく薔薇の枝などありえようか。画家の創りものでなくて何であろう。

現代の画家たちは、写実主義がひとつのイリュージョンにしか過ぎぬことをよく知っている。ランピネーリはここに、現実と見せかけながら実は「静物画」として知られている絵画のひとつのシンボルを創りだしているのである。「静物画 NATURA MORTA」とは「死した自然」のことであって、元来、人間のメランコリーを誘発する人間の創りものに他ならなかったのである。

1 "Still Life" 「静物」 1990

2 "Still Life"「静物」1989

3 "Still Life" 「静物」 1989

4 "Still Life" 「静物」 1988

5 "Still Life" 「静物」 1989

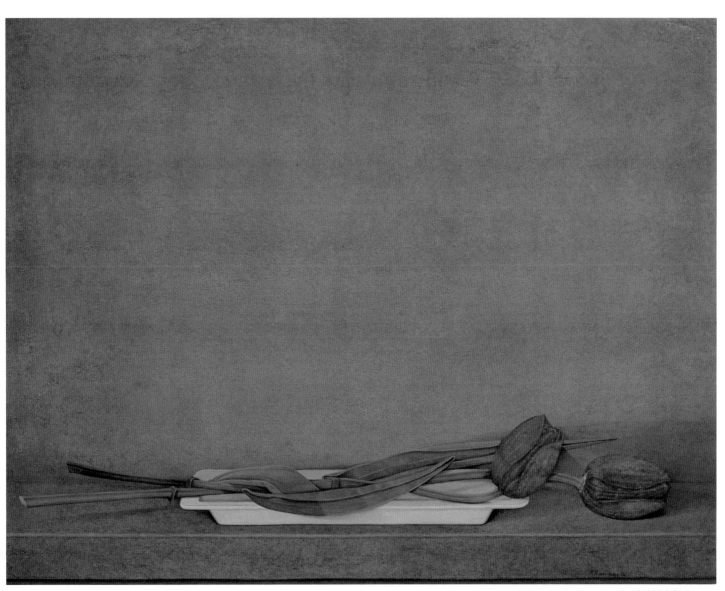

6 "Still Life" 「静物」 1989

7 "Still Life" 「静物」 1989

8 "Still Life" 「静物」 1990

9 "Still Life" 「静物」 1989

10 "Still Life" 「静物」 1990

11 "Still Life" 「静物」 1991

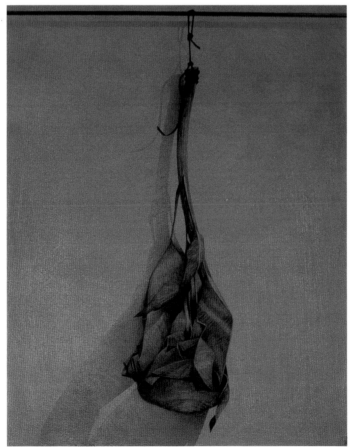

12 "Still Life" 「静物」 1989

13 "Still Life" 「静物」 1989

14 "Still Life"「静物」1990

15 "Still Life"「静物」1990

16　"Still Life"「静物」1990

17 "Still Life" 「静物」 1989

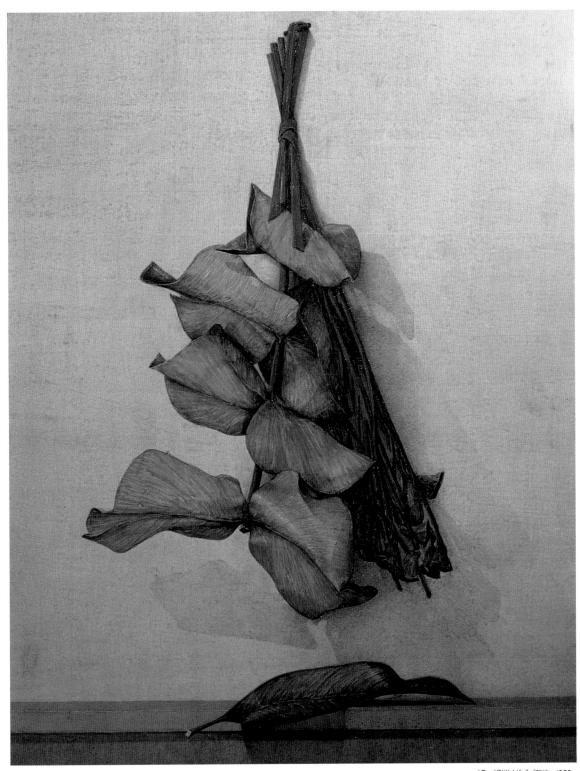

18 "Still Life" 「静物」 1989

DUGALD STERMER ドゥガルド・スターマー

Steven Heller スティーブン・ヘラー

Twenty years ago Dugald Stermer was such an accomplished art director that at the time it seemed foolhardy for him to switch his focus from design to illustration. Stermer's gift for making striking magazine formats was legend. His layout for *Ramparts* magazine was classical yet fresh, quiet though vigorous. He could get the most interesting, often acerbic, artwork from many, some quite renowned, illustrators. But Stermer, a frustrated illustrator himself, was not completely satisfied with his accomplishments. When he took a hiatus from art direction, the pressing question among those who knew him was, "Could Stermer be a credible illustrator?"

Stermer initially developed a rather flat, poster style of portraiture consistent with the prevailing preference for illustration to be graphic, colorful, yet void of expression. He sold a couple to *Time* magazine and did some advertising, but for the most part this daring foray into the marketplace was a failure, and so he wisely returned to designing magazines.

Fortuitously one of his clients, *Oceans* magazine, offered him an opportunity to experiment with a new illustration approach. Thereafter Stermer shed his contricting style for another that was remarkably fluid. Instead of gouache he turned to pencils and water colors. Rejecting lifeless portraits he began to render, in the tradition of the 19th century naturalists, exquisite drawings of exotic flora and fauna. One of his first assignments was to draw some of the animal kingdom's least attractive creatures, snails and slugs. Owing to the requirement that they be biologically accurate, it would have been a difficult assignment for even the seasoned naturalist; but for this neophyte the result was a masterpiece of picture making to the point that these otherwise slimy critters were made quite appealing.

Today, though he does not consider himself a nature specialist, Stermer is probably one of the most prolific artists in this field. Naturalist illustration was also a key to becoming more involved with general, editorial illustration. As an art director Stermer was not just an aesthetistician, but a conceptualist with the talent to make the most complex ideas into accessible images. As an illustrator he often weds technical proficiency to conceptual acuity in ways that the cartoonist/illustrator can only touch upon. He is so adept at rendering the real that when his images are surreal one is not conscious of the illusion so much as accepting of a peculiar, yet decidedly credible vision.

Stermer is 54 and his work reflects the experience that comes from his years. Of course, when compared to trendy young illustrators—the ones who have rejected formalism for "pure expression"—Stermer's art might seem to have the musty aura of anachronism, but nothing can be further from the truth. Indeed, classical approaches to art are not old-fashioned but timeless. And Stermer has purposely chosen to use a time-honored means to express timely issues.

Stermer is no stranger to rebellion. Years ago he made classical magazine design a viable option. Now he is living proof that intelligent, craft-driven illustration is a necessary alternative to stylistic contortionism.

ドゥガルド・スターマーは20年前、アートディレクターとして既に成功していた。彼のエディトリアルデザインの才能は伝説的であり、例えば『ランパーツ』誌のレイアウトは古典的でありながら新鮮で、落ち着きがありながら迫力があった。彼はアートディレクターとして多くの有名なイラストレーターに興味深い、時には難しい作品を作らせることができたが、それらに満足できず、自ら描きたいという欲求にかられ、デザインからイラストレーションへと転向した。当時このことは非常に無謀に思え、彼を知る人々の間では「スターマーはイラストレーターとして成功するだろうか」という疑問がもちあがった。

スターマーは最初、当時流行していた写実的でカラフルだが、表情に乏しい単調な肖像画風のイラストレーションを描いていた。そして彼は『タイム』誌に売り込んで広告の制作をしたものの、この分野への大胆な進出は失敗に終わったため、再びエディトリアルデザイナーに戻ってしまった。

幸運にも彼のクライアントである『オーシャンズ』誌が、新しい手法を試みる機会を提供してくれた。以来、彼は抑制されたスタイルを流動的なものに、ガッシュを鉛筆と水彩に変えた。そして生彩を欠く肖像画を捨て、19世紀の自然主義者にならい、珍しい動植物の細密画を描き始めたのである。最初の題材は、動物界ではあまり目立たないカタツムリやナメクジであった。生物学的に細密な描写が求められていたので、専門家でさえ難しい仕事であったに違いない。しかし、ネバネバした気持ちの悪い動物がとても魅力的に描かれ最高の出来となった。今日、彼に自然専門家という自覚はないが、おそらくこの分野においては最も多作の芸術家の一人であろう。

この自然主義者の作品が普通のエディトリアルイラストレーションに関わるきっかけともなった。アートディレクターとしてのスターマーは単なる美学者ではなく、複雑な概念をわかりやすいイメージに表すことの出来る概念論者である。イラストレーターとしての彼は技術と概念的な鋭さを結びつけ、漫画家、イラストレーター顔負けの作品を作っている。彼の作品は実にリアルであるため、たとえそれが超現実的なものであっても、見る者は気づかずに、異常な、しかし説得力あるその絵を受け入れてしまう。

スターマーは現在54歳、彼の作品には年齢ゆえの経験が表れている。「純粋表現」のための形式主義を嫌う流行の若手作家に比べると、陳腐で時代遅れに見えるかも知れないが決してそうではない。古典的手法は時代遅れではなく、時代を越えて魅力的だ。スターマーはあえて伝統的な方法を選びその時代にあったテーマを表現しているのだ。

スターマーは抵抗を知らないわけではない。何年も昔に彼は古典的なエディトリアルデザインを価値あるひとつの選択肢にした。そして今、彼は知的で技術指向のイラストレーションが、形式偏重主義に代わる、もうひとつの選択であることを証明しているのである。

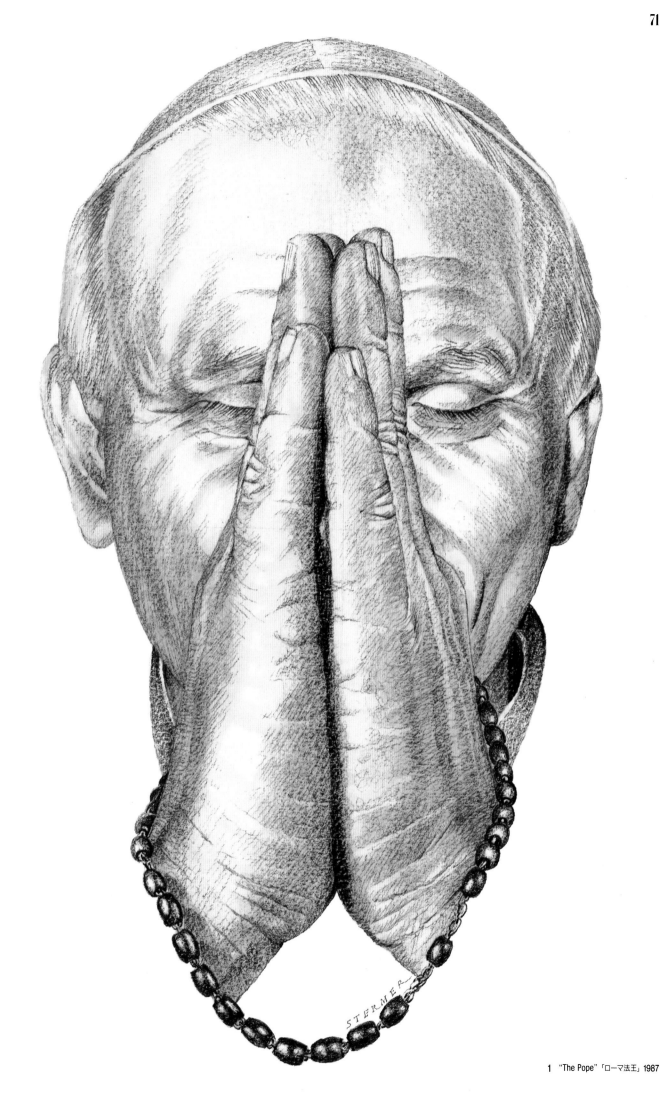

1 "The Pope" 「ローマ法王」 1987

STERMER

2 "Jane Goodall" 「ジェーン・グッドオール」 1989

3 "Lilac and Flag" 「ライラックと旗」 1990

4 Catalog cover カタログの表紙 1987

EAGLE'S CLAW CACTUS

Echinocactus horizonthalonius var. nicholii

6

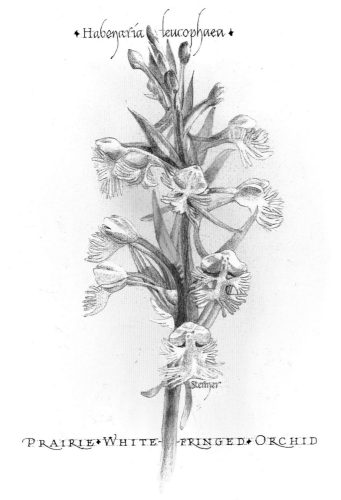

* Habenaria leucophaea *

Stermer

PRAIRIE•WHITE—FRINGED•ORCHID

5

Chrysosplenium
iowense

Stermer

GOLDEN • SAXIFRAGE

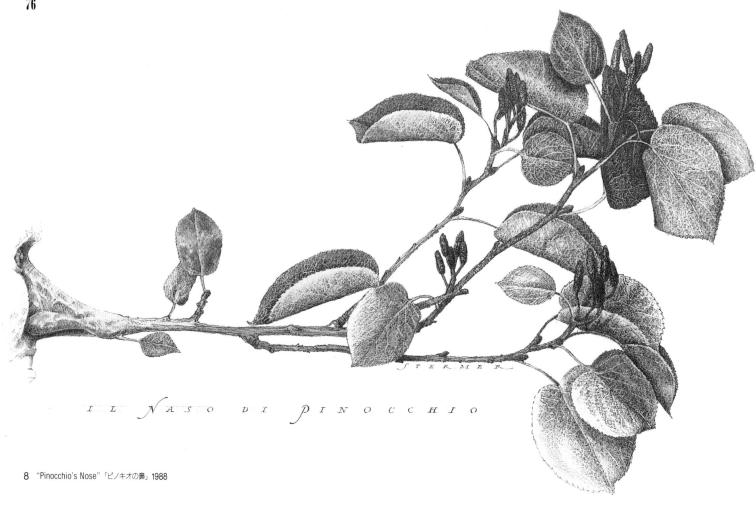

I L   N A S O   D I   P I N O C C H I O

8 "Pinocchio's Nose" 「ピノキオの鼻」 1988

LEAVES are food factories for trees. Leaf cells contain clorophyll, which uses sunlight & moisture to change carbon dioxide & chemicals into sugar.

Brown leaves, as in some of the oaks, are caused by substances called tannins.

Yellow & Orange pigments are called caroteyes & xanthophylls. Seen in such trees as birches, & hickories, it is the same pigment found in carrots, butter & daffodils.

Red & Purple are caused by antocyanyn in some trees. The same pigment is found in Concord grapes & cranberries.

Cell layer forms at the base of each leaf where it is attached to the twig sealing off the flow of moisture to the leaf. The time of colorful fall foliage is about two weeks after the layer forms. Another layer of cells grows in beneath this, like scar tissue, to cover the wound when the leaf falls.

Clorophyll makes leaves green. It also masks yellows that are there all the time, hidden by the green. When the flow of moisture stops, clorophyll is not renewed and underlying colors are revealed. Each species has its own chemical makeup, which gives many color variations.

9 "Leaf" 「葉」 1988

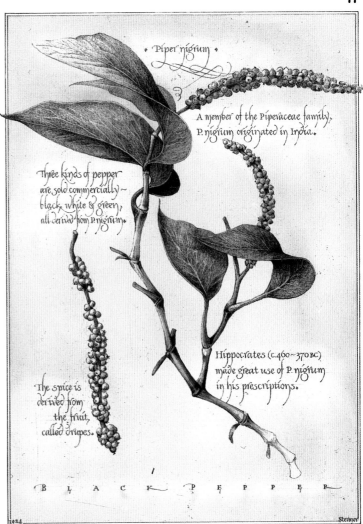

11 "Black Pepper"「黒胡椒」1984

10 "The Yellow Rose of Texas"「テキサス産黄バラ」1987

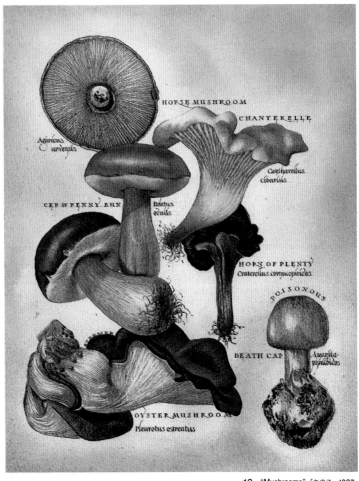

12 "Mushrooms"「きのこ」1987

13　Magazine illustration　雑誌のイラストレーション　1988

14 "Birds of America" 「アメリカの鳥」1989

15 "Endangered Species" 「危機に瀕する種」1990

Tyto alba

Length: 36 ~ 51 centimeters

Barn owls are extremely efficient nocturnal hunters, capable of taking many rodents, such as mice and rats. They live in tropical and temperate climates on all continents.

Lays 5 ~ 11 round, white eggs

STERMER

B A R N · O W L

16   "Barn Owl" 「メンフクロウ」 1991

This albatross is the largest species in its family, and the longest-winged of all birds.

Wingspan: 290~324 cm.

Diomedea exulans
WANDERING
ALBATROSS

STERMER

18 "Wandering Albatross" 「ワタリアホウドリ」 1989

PEREGRINE FALCON

Falco peregrinus

STERMER

17 "Peregrine Falcon" 「ハヤブサ」 1990

VANISHING SONGBIRDS ◆ FINE ART OF WALKING

SIERRA

MARCH/APRIL 1986 $2.50

19 Magazine cover 雑誌の表紙 1986

MAURITIAN
PALM

Sterner

· Hyophorbe · amaricaulis ·

20 "Vanishing Flora"「滅びゆく植物」1987

CHAMELEON

In addition to their ability to change color
in order to match the surrounding foliage,
the 80 or so species of chameleons
have coiled prehensile tails,
eyes that turn & focus sepa-
rately, & toes arranged
in opposed groups of
twos and threes.

· Chamaeleo bitaeniatus ·

· Chamaeleo owenii ·

21 "Chameleon"「カメレオン」1990

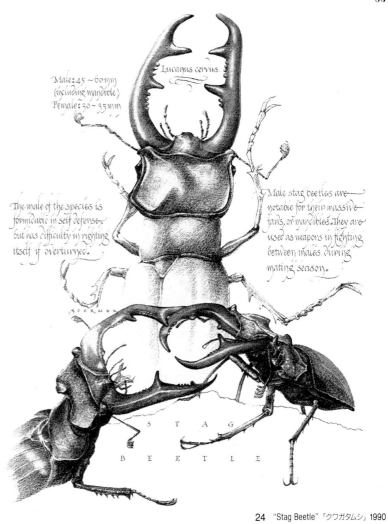

Male: 45 ~ 60mm
(including mandible)
Female: 30 ~ 35mm

Lucanus cervus.

The male of the species is formidable in self defense but has difficulty in righting itself if overturned.

Male stag beetles are notable for their massive jaws, or mandibles. They are used as weapons in fighting between males during mating season.

24 "Stag Beetle" 「クワガタムシ」 1990

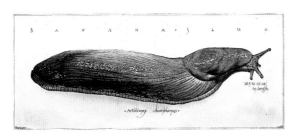

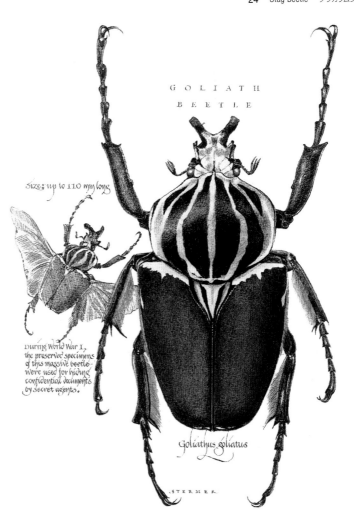

GOLIATH
BEETLE

Size; up to 110 mm long

During World War I, the preserved specimens of this massive beetle were used for hiding confidential documents by secret agents.

Goliathus goliatus

22 "Snail" 「カタツムリ」 1991   23 "Banana Slug" 「ナメクジ」 1984   25 "Goliath Beetle" 「ゴライアスオオツノコガネ」 1989

· M A N A T E E ·

STERMER

Length: to 460 cm
Weight: to 874 kg

Trichichus manatus latirostris

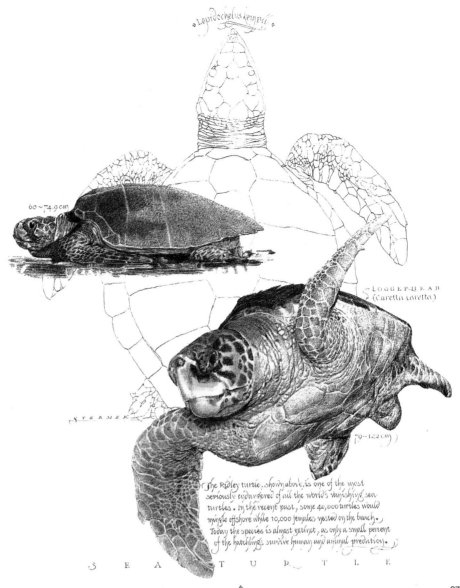

Lepidochelus kempii

60~74.9 cm

LOGGERHEAD
(Caretta caretta)

STERMER

70~122 cm

The Ridley turtle, shown above, is one of the most seriously endangered of all the world's vanishing sea turtles. In the recent past, some 40,000 turtles would mingle offshore while 10,000 females nested on the beach. Today the species is almost extinct, as only a small percent of the hatchlings survive human and animal predation.

S E A T U R T L E

27 "Sea Turtle"「ウミガメ」1990

C A L I F O R N I A
S E A L I O N

Stermer

Zalophus californianus

28 "California Sea Lion"「クロアシカ」1988

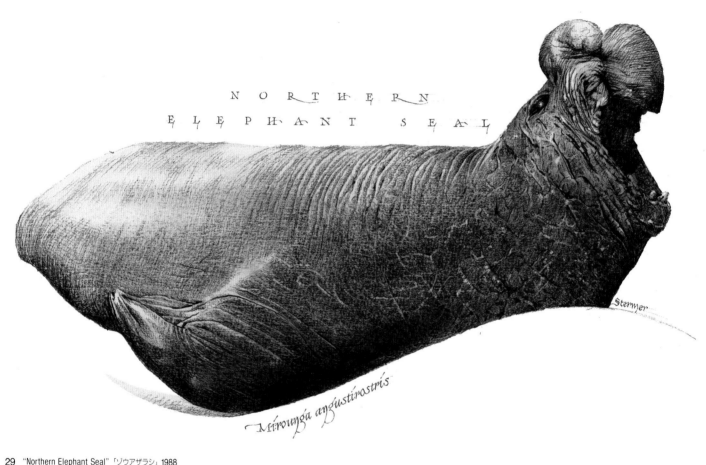

NORTHERN
ELEPHANT SEAL

Mirounga angustirostris

29 "Northern Elephant Seal"「ゾウアザラシ」1988

Phoca vitulina

HARBOR SEAL
[nursing]

30 "Harbor Seal"「ゴマフアザラシ」1988

31 "Orca" 「シャチ」 1987

Panthera tigris sumatrae

WEIGHT
Male: 220 ~ 308 lbs
Female: 165 ~ 242 lbs

LENGTH
Head to tail: 7.2 ~ 8.9 feet

SUMATRAN · TIGER

33 "Cheetah" 「チータ」 1987

34 "Snow Leopard" 「ユキヒョウ」 1990

35 "Grizzly Bear" 「ハイイログマ」 1984

36 "Brown Hare" 「ノウサギ」 1991

Canis lupus   Stermer 1984

37 "Wolf" 「オオカミ」 1984

W H I T E   R A T

38 "White Rat" 「シロネズミ」 1988

SHIN MATSUNAGA 松永 真

Mamoru Yonekura 米倉 守

Beauty, I believe, is a phenomenon that innately requires no ostentatious display, no stentorian trumpeting. On the contrary, true beauty should be tranquil, almost inconspicuous, like a pleasing silence. The works of Shin Matsunaga have much in common with these sentiments of mine: with their airy spatial configurations, their aura is one of peaceful tranquility...like an open plot of land in the middle of a raucous and bustling city.

Man tends to regard artistic beauty as something which should be gravely profound, unwaveringly firm, immovable, powerful, eternal. Viewing the works of Shin Matsunaga, I cannot but feel however that this notion is fundamentally wrong.

Matsunaga's works are, for a fact, laid out with stalwart assurance. Yet rather than giving them an air of grave profundity—like an oak tree rooted firmly in the ground and reaching high toward the heavens—the solidity of his works imbues them with a marvelously supple lightness.

The poet Makoto Ooka wrote a verse to the following effect: "Ladle out the oceans' waters as one might, Soar through the skies as high as one might, Nowhere is there a trace of that deep, deep blue. The waters are clear; The sky is transparent. / Blue lies beyond the horizon of reality, for it is the color of light. We speak of 'blue flowers,' flowers of a hue we but long for. We speak of 'bluebirds of happiness,' birds that do not exist."

The transparently clear works of Shin Matsunaga, in a manner so much like this poem, use celestial and aquatic colors to transform the bluebirds of our imagination into visual realities. They are unassuming, tranquil, clear. They possess an air of infinite freedom—a sense found in all great works of art—that lightens the burdens of their beholders.

While the majority of contemporary design works, with their conscious attempts to evoke emotions, strength or splendor, make me suffocate, the works of Shin Matsunaga allow me to breathe. This is because they are infused with an extra layer of air, a ripple of wind, a sense of lighthearted freedom of a kind man was inherently created to possess. Matsunaga's eyes reach to every nook, like a wind that never ceases to blow, without beginning or end, defying capture in any framework or receptacle. Life, I believe, is like this also. And it is for this reason that I see Shin Matsunaga's graphic creations as works to enhance the crossbreezes of our lives.

The Chinese philosopher Lao-zi taught that "great works need no embellishment." By this he meant that works of true greatness need no additions or alterations in any way. Art, therefore, is inherently unfinished. The best works never reach completion; they are not embellished with affectations of eccentric uniqueness or lofty wisdom. They are like the universe, the grandest phenomenon known to man: they are intrinsically lacking in form. This formlessness is an integral element of Oriental art.

Shin Matsunaga's works are sustained by his unaffected individuality...an individuality as expansive as the sky, as profound as the oceans.

美しさ、というものは本来ものものしさ、とか声高なものは必要としないのではないかと思う。それれは静かなもので、むしろ目ざわりにならないもの、という感じを私は持っている。小気味よい沈黙。デザインの空間と自分の気分が通じ合う松永真の仕事は、騒々しい都会の中で自分だけの空間を見つけたような静けさがある。

亀倉雄策は「Vision of Water」などの作品を例にその清涼感を指摘していたが、私も松永作品のかんどころは「色即是空」ではなく「空即是色」だと見てきた。

人は芸術美などというと、重厚なもの、確固たるもの、不動のもの、力強いもの、永遠的なものをもとめるが、これも根本的に間違ってはいないか、と私は松永真の作品をみてそう思うのである。

松永真の画面構成はがっちりと仕上げられている。まさにそのことが、大地に根を張って天に伸びるケヤキの樹のように重厚を感じさせる代りに軽さを感じさせるのだ。

大岡信の詩の一節。「海の水をいくらすくってみても、空高くいかに舞い上がってみても、深々とたたへてゐた青の色はどこにもない。水は透明、空も透明。

青の色はまことに現実の彼方の色。それは光の色だからだ。『青い花』、『青い鳥』。憧れの色、ゐない鳥。」

この詩のように松永真の極めて透明感の強い作品群は、天上の色、水上の色を駆使して、青い鳥、ゐない鳥を現実、視覚化しているのである。さりげなく、静かで透明。見るものの気持を軽くするその限りない自由な感じ、この感じこそすべての偉大な芸術に備わっているものである。

感動を、力強さを、華やかさを感じさせようとする現代のデザインの前で私は窒息するが、松永真の前ではほっと呼吸してしまうという具合である。なぜならそこには空気の層があり、風の波紋があり、自由の感じがあるからだろう。人間本来の「軽さ」の表現といってもよい。

松永真の目は、風のようにどんな片隅にも入りこみながらどこにも停止せず、始めも終りもなく、いかなる枠、容器にもとらえられないものである。私は人生もまたそのようなもの、と心している。だから松永の作品は人生や社会の風通しをよくするための仕事にほかならない、と受け取っている。

大制無割……大制は割くことなし、と老子はいう。大制つまり最上の作品は、決して割いたり、刻んだりして手を加えないもの。人間も最上の人物は、知識などで飾ったり小細工したりしたものではない。例の「大器晩成」も大器という最大の作品は、何も手を加えない素純のもの、できあがらないという意味がほんとうだという。

美術とは本来どこまでいっても未完成であるのだ。だから最上のものはついに出来上がらないもの、さかしらの個性とか知識で飾らないものということになる。たとえば宇宙は最大の現象であるが、それに形はない。無形に対する考え方、感じ方は必ず東洋の美に影を映しているが、なまじの個性など考えない個性こそ松永真の根本を支えているものだと思う。空のように、水のように。

松永真の特異な造形骨格は大制無割である。

ORCHESTRA FESTIVAL

1 Concert poster 音楽会のポスター 1991

2   Poster on theme of "Water" 「水」をテーマにしたポスター 1989

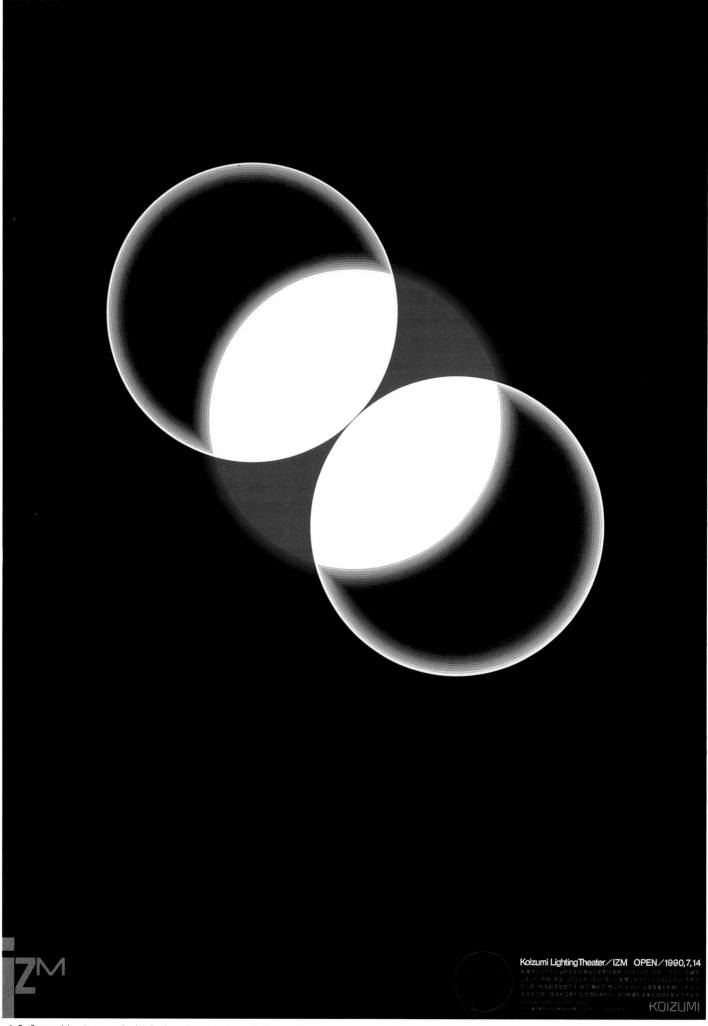

Koizumi LightingTheater／IZM OPEN／1990,7,14

4-6　Commercial posters promoting interior decor shop　インテリアショップのポスター　1990

5

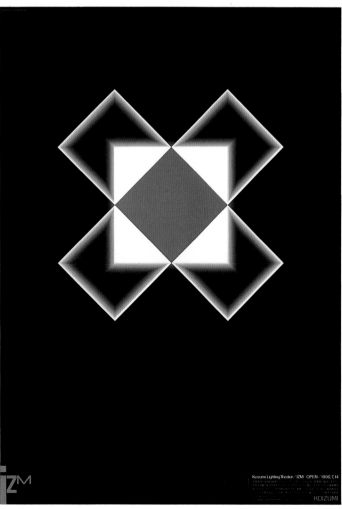

7

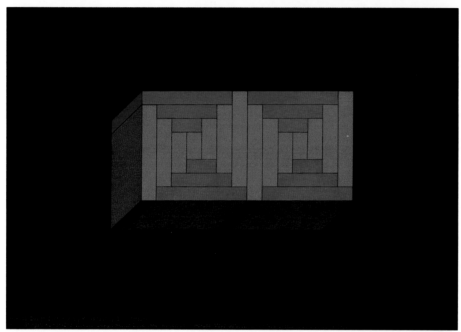

8

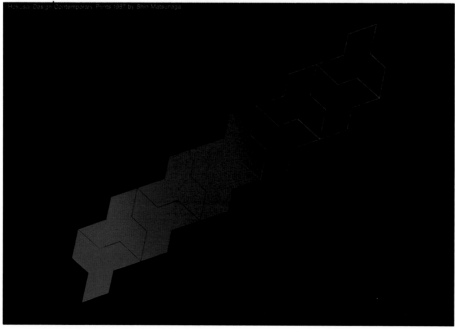

7-9 Prints patterned after Hokusai 北斎パターンによる版画 1987

'91 JAPAN SHOP

10　Poster for trade fair on shop interior decoration　店舗見本市のポスター　1991

11

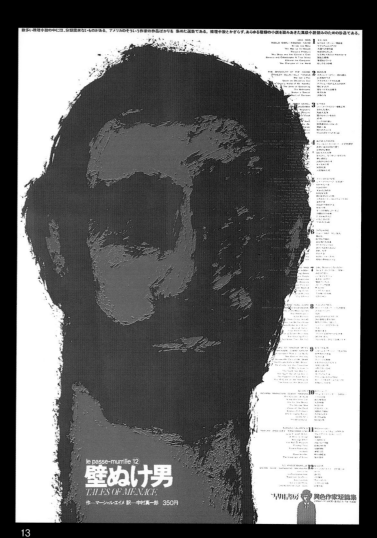

13

11-13　Trilogy of posters promoting book of special exhibition works　展覧会出品の書籍ポスター3部作　1967

Travel, and Educate Yourself!
"Communication Brings Peace"

PEACE
Joining Hiroshima Appeals 1988
Design & Illustration by Shin Matsunaga

15　Peace poster　平和ポスター　1988

P E A C E

LOVE, PEACE, AND HAPPINESS.
Joining "HIROSHIMA APPEALS 1986" / Design & Illustration by Shin Matsunaga

14　Peace poster　平和ポスター　1986

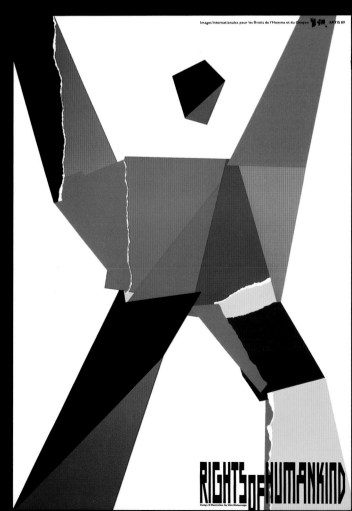

Images Internationales pour les Droits de l'Homme et du Citoyen　ARTIS 89

RIGHTS OF HUMANKIND
Design & Illustration by Shin Matsunaga

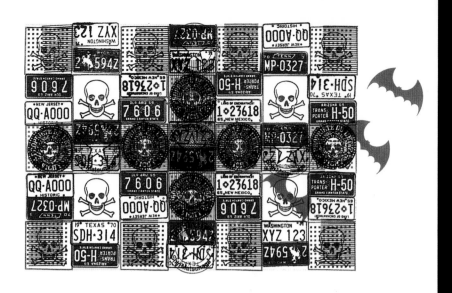

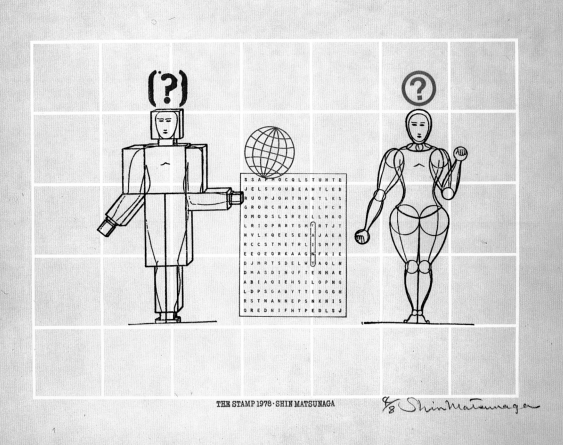

THE STAMP 1978 · SHIN MATSUNAGA

21 Postcard promoting exhibition 展覧会のポストカード 1978

22　Poster promoting interior decor trade fair　インテリア見本市のポスター　1991

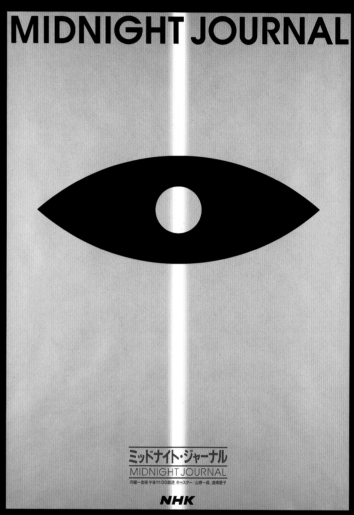

24　Poster for TV program　テレビ番組のポスター　1990

25 Peace poster 平和ポスター 1985

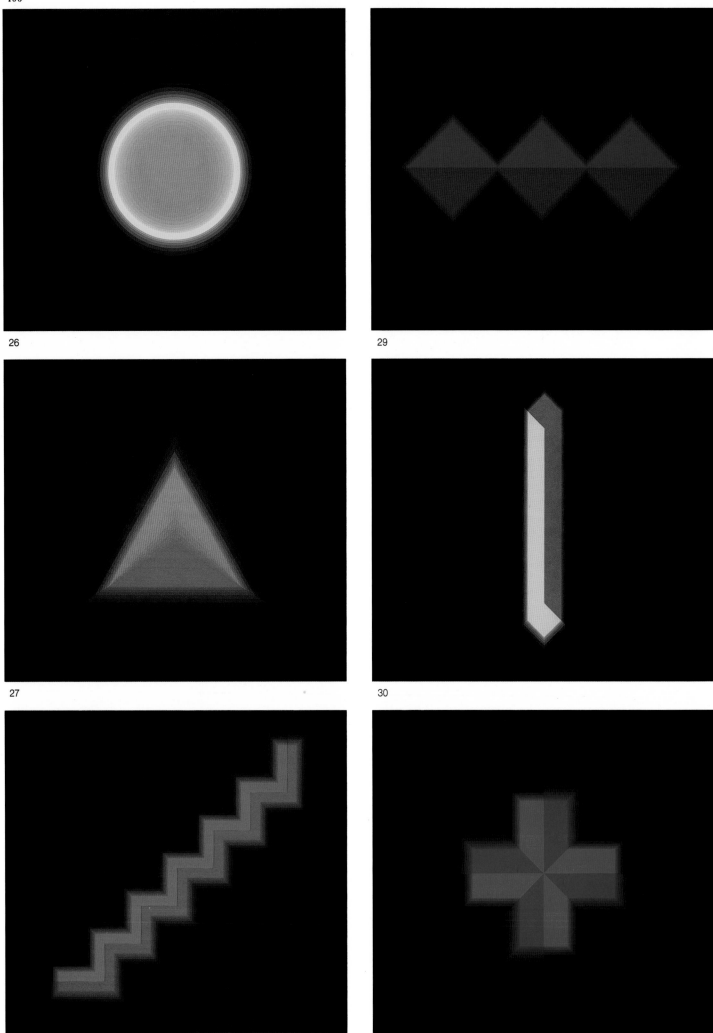

26

27

29

30

31

26-31 Calendar designs カレンダーのビジュアル 1989

32　Poster for design conference　デザイン会議のポスター　1989

33　Poster announcing one-man show　個展ポスター　1988

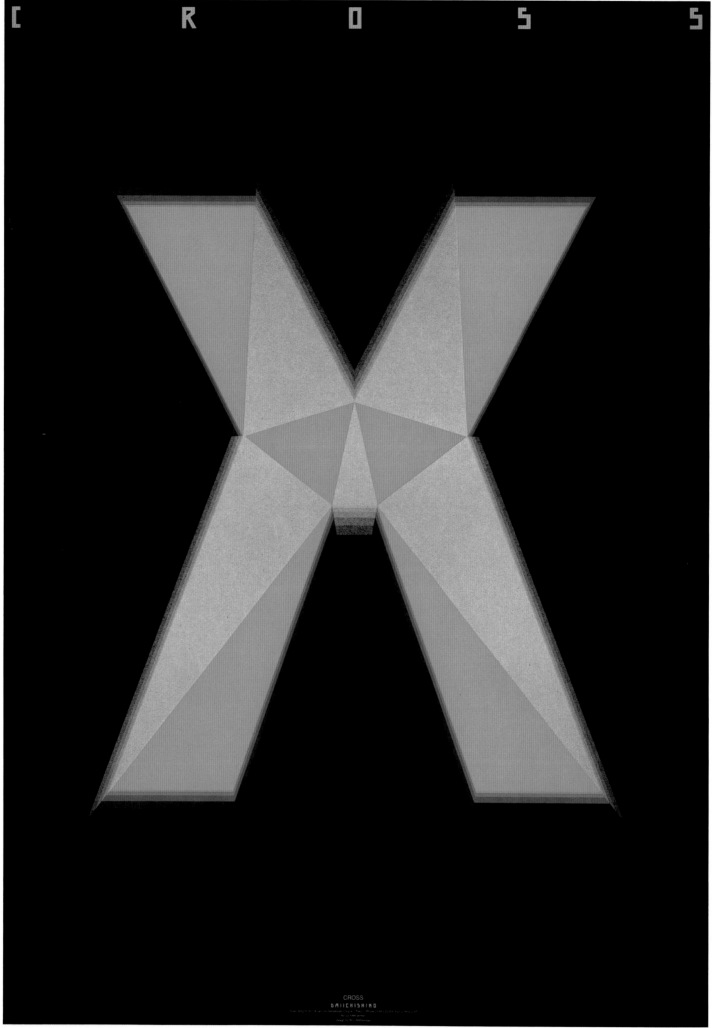

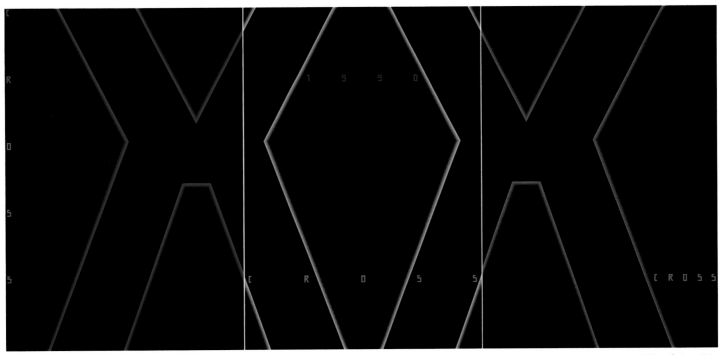

35 Commercial posters for planning - and - printing company 企画・印刷会社のポスター 1990

36 Commercial poster for planning - and - printing company 企画・印刷会社のポスター 1991

Individual Realities in the California Art Scene

Peter Alexander
Carlos Almaraz
Tony Berlant
Laurie Brown
David Bunn
Jo Ann Callis
Suzanne Caporael
Karen Carson
Eileen Cowin
John Divola
Brad Durham
Llyn Foulkes
John Frame
Charles Garabedian
Jill Giegerich
D. J. Hall
Roger Herman
Anthony Hernandez
David Hockney
Mike Kelly
Mark Lere
Michael C. McMillen
Gwynn Murrill
Manuel Ocampo
Liga Pang
Roland Reiss
Bruce Richards
Ilene Segalove
Peter Shelton
George Stone
Jon Swihart
Mitchell Syrop
Joyce Treiman
Bill Viola
Tom Wudl
Bruce and Norman Yonemoto
Peter Zokosky

カリフォルニア アート・シーン
自然、生活と創造のなかのリアリティー

主催 セゾン美術館、カリフォルニア・インター
ナショナル・アーツ・ファンデーション、毎日新聞社
後援 外務省、文化庁、アメリカ大使館、ロサン
ジェルス市文化事業部 協力 ソニー株式会社

1991年5月11日(土) 6月10日(月)

セゾン美術館
SEZON MUSEUM OF ART

入場料 一般1000円(900円)、大・高生800円(700円)
中・小生300円(200円) ( )内は前売り・団体20名以上(消費税込み)
セゾン美術館(東京・池袋)03・5992・8700
午前10時 午後8時(受付は午後7時30分まで) 火曜休室

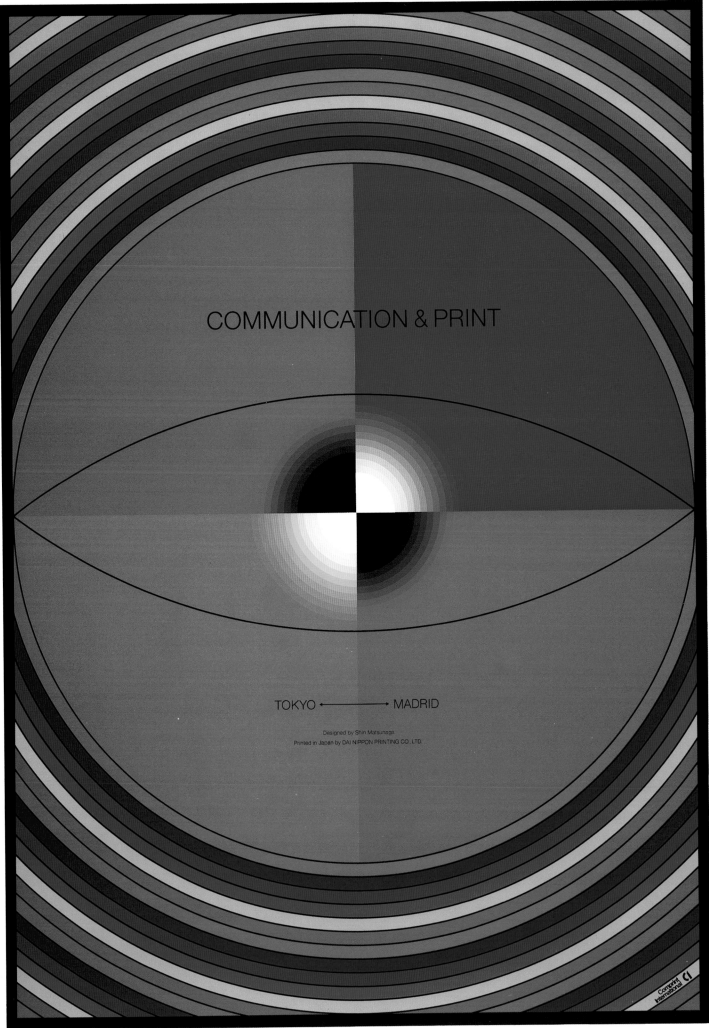

WIKTOR SADOWSKI ヴィクトル・サドフスキ

Noboru Matsuura 松浦 昇

When he captured the Gold Medal in the Cultural Division at the International Poster Biennale in Warsaw in 1984, Wiktor Sadowski was but three years fresh from graduating from that city's Academy of Fine Arts. His victory in this most competitive of all divisions—accomplished with the poster "Goya: A Night at the Ballet" (1983), which was only his fourth work to date at the time—was greeted with great surprise not only by the citizens of Warsaw but, perhaps even more so, by Sadowski himself. After this stunning debut, Sadowski was offered a flood of commercial contracts. He selected his jobs prudently, however, making every effort to avoid falling into a trap of narcissism or self-complacency.

Sadowski's brilliant artistic talents, his refined technical skills and his penetrating powers of perception are often said to be reminiscent of the young Franciszek Starowieyski, whose influence is seen in Sadowski's "Goya" poster as well as in his "Yerma: A Night at the Ballet" (1983). Personally, while I would not deny Starowieyski's influence, I wish to stress instead what I perceive to be influences from the Dutch school. Whereas Starowieyski betrays influences of baroque artistry blended with an admixture of Latin traits, Sadowski shares the Germanic, nonsensuous, spiritual aura of Dutch painting. The two artists are alike, undeniably however, in their astonishing talent, and their works are equally replete with ideas of imaginative richness.

Among Dutch artists, Sadowski has a special fondness for Hieronymus Bosch and Pieter Bruegel. From Bosch he learned the artistry of unique design form; from Bruegel he learned how to observe everyday life with open-minded honesty and humor. Sadowski then blended these elements to create a grammar of form resplendent in wit. He contrasts with Bosch's unique originality, though, in being an avid proponent (along with Starowieyski, Jan Jaromir Aleksiun and Jerzy Czerniawski) of the "grotesque," a Polish style of healthy humor and caricature that takes its viewers by surprise with a surrealistic technique. Where Sadowski manifests his uncommon powers of perception is in the way he captures his characters in the split second of an expressive moment, paying heed to correlations between parts yet ignoring matters of detail.

After his fellow citizens began to recognize the great expanse and richness of his creative talents, Sadowski came to feel the heavy burden of their expectations. For a time his creative genius reached a deepening impasse, and to elude it Sadowski left Poland in 1988 for two years of study in the United States. He returned home in 1990, just days before the start of the 13th Warsaw Biennale.

What Sadowski pondered and learned in the U.S. will become known to us only through the works which he will reveal to us in the years ahead. Yet whatever the outcome, he will unquestionably be destined to carry on the tradition of the Polish poster. For Wiktor Sadowski, an artist of outstanding substance like so many of his compatriots before him, clearly occupies an important position in the poster artistry of his country in the post-war era.

第9・10回ワルシャワ国際ポスタービエンナーレの文化ポスター部門において、まだ、ワルシャワ美術アカデミーを卒業して3年しか経っていないヴィクトル・サドフスキが制作したポスター『ゴヤ』バレエの夕べ (1983年) が、金賞を受賞した。このポスターは彼にとって第4作目であるが、ワルシャワ・コンペの最も競争が激しい文化ポスター部門におけるこの決定は、市民やサドフスキ自身に驚きをもって迎えられた。このような衝撃的デビューを果したサドフスキは、ビエンナーレ後、たくさんの注文を受けるようになったが、慎重に仕事を選択し、自己満足や自己陶酔に陥らないように努めた。

彼の芸術における才気のひらめきや技巧、そして深い洞察力は、若きフランチシェク・スタロヴェイスキを想起させ、ポスター『ゴヤ』や『イエーマ』バレエの夕べ (1983年) は、まさにスタロヴェイスキの影響が指摘されている。私は、スタロヴェイスキの影響を否定しないが、よりネーデルランド絵画からの影響を強調したい。すなわち、スタロヴェイスキの個性はバロック芸術から影響を受け、ラテン的なものが混合しているが、サドフスキの個性はネーデルランド絵画からの影響によって非感覚的、精神的で、ゲルマン的なものが混合している、といえる。しかし、芸術における目のさめるような才気のひらめきは、共通しており、彼らの絵の中に織り込まれた思想は、豊かな想像力に満ちている。

サドフスキは、ネーデルランド絵画の中でも、特に、ハンス・メムリンクや、ヒエロニムス・ボッス、ピーテル・ブリューゲルが、お気に入りの画家である。確かにネーデルランド絵画に通じる明暗法がみられるが、彼は、明暗と光と空気を、さまざまな空間内でうまく関連づけている。そして、ボッスの個性的な造形、ブリューゲルの先入観のない誠実さとユーモアによる日常の人間生活の観察を学び、機知豊かに造形文法を形成していった、といえる。

また、ボッスの独創性と対峙されるスタロヴェイスキや、ヤン・ヤロミル・アレクシュン、イエジィ・チェルニアフスキの手法——シュールリアリズム的手法に人々の意表をつく"グロテスク"は、ポーランド流の健全なユーモアとカリカチュアであり、サドフスキはその手法を強く意識している。彼が描く人物は、表情の動きを瞬時に捉え、部分部分の相互関係に注意し、細部を無視する大胆さは、彼の直観する能力の非凡さを示している。

市民は、彼の創造力の広大さ、豊かさを十分認識しはじめ、彼は、その期待の重さに悩み、一時期、創作活動が停滞した。それから逃避するかのように、1988年から2年間、アメリカ留学に旅立ち、1990年、第13回ワルシャワ国際ポスタービエンナーレ開会の数日前に帰国した。アメリカで彼が何を考え、何を学んだかは、今後の作品を通して理解する以外にない。しかし、彼はポーランドポスターの伝統を受け継ぐ宿命を負わされている。彼を、戦後から今日までのポーランドポスターと並べて置けば、ポーランドポスター芸術の流れにおいて本質的なものが際立ち、彼の存在が重要な位置をしめていることは、明白である。

Teatr Dramatyczny 1986

Oldřich Daněk

A jednak powrócę...

SADOWSKI 86

1 Theater poster 劇場ポスター 1986

XXV
Rzeszowskie
Spotkania
Teatralne

czerwiec
1986

2 Theater poster 劇場ポスター 1986

3 Poster promoting printing company 印刷会社のポスター 1990

4 Theater poster 劇場ポスター 1991

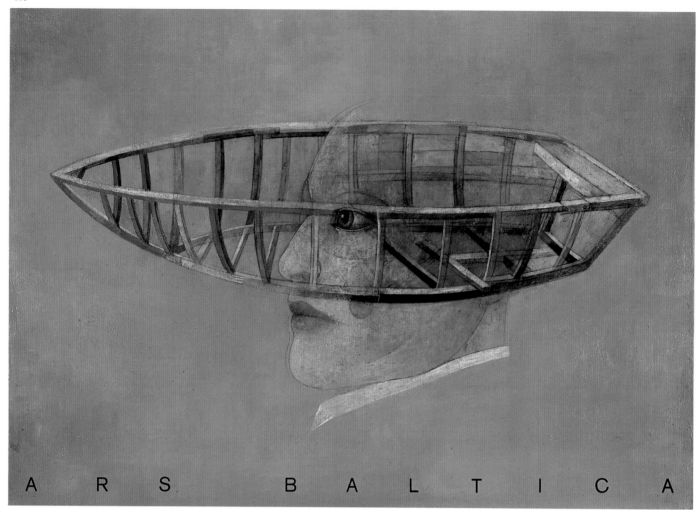

5   Exhibition poster 展覧会ポスター 1991

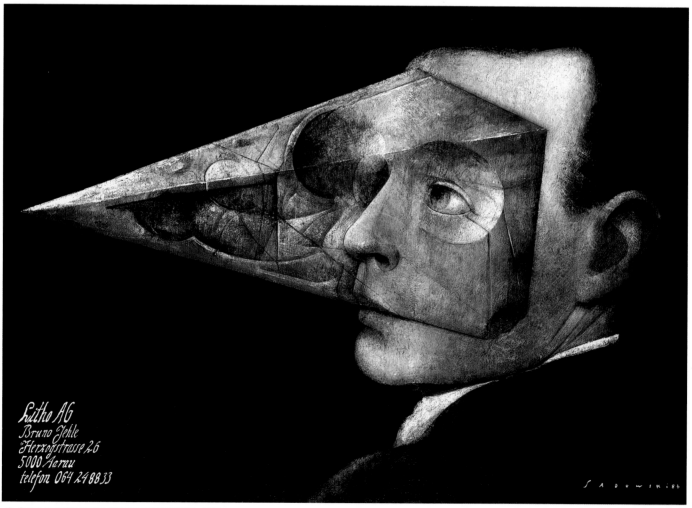

6   Poster promoting printing company 印刷会社のポスター 1987

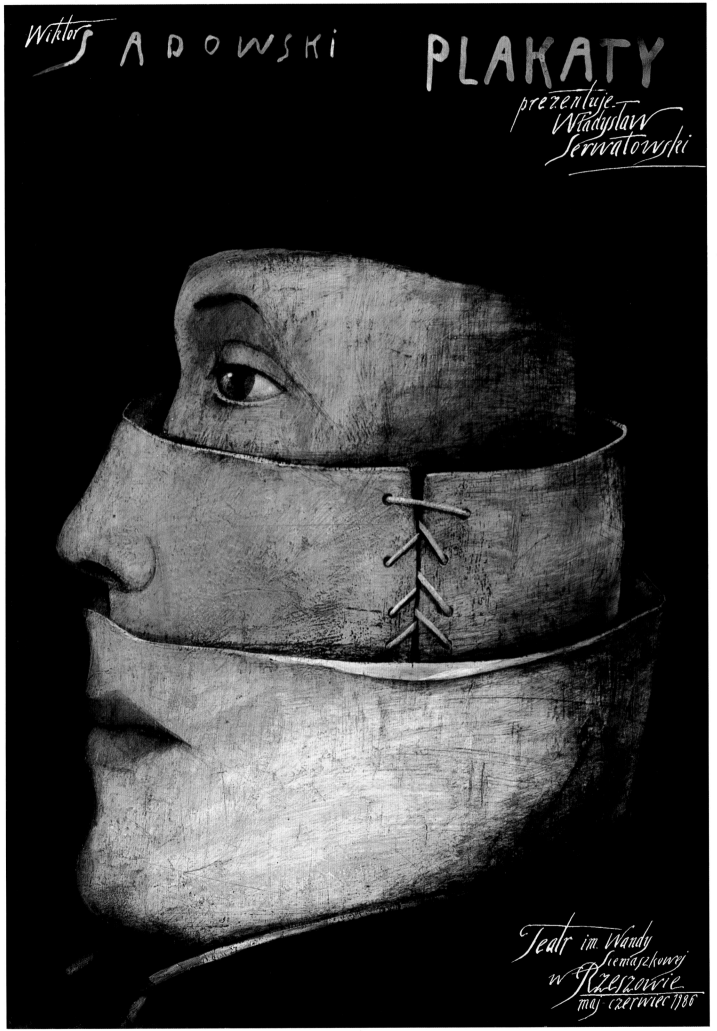

7 Poster promoting one-man show 個展ポスター 1986

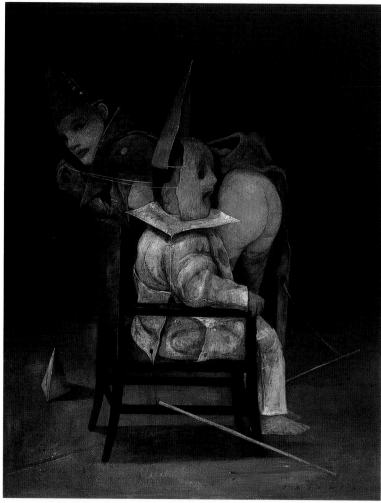

8

10 Exhibition poster 展覧会ポスター 1986

8-9 "Oleandry" paintings 「オレアンドリー」 ペインティング 1988

11 "Oleandry" painting 「オレアンドリー」 ペインティング 1988

12 "The Book" drawing 「本」ドローイング 1989

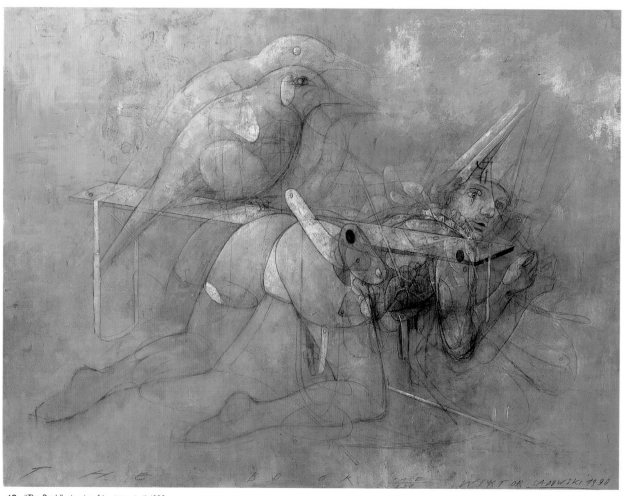

13 "The Book" drawing 「本」ドローイング 1990

14 "The Book" drawing 「本」ドローイング 1989

15 "The Book" drawing 「本」ドローイング 1991

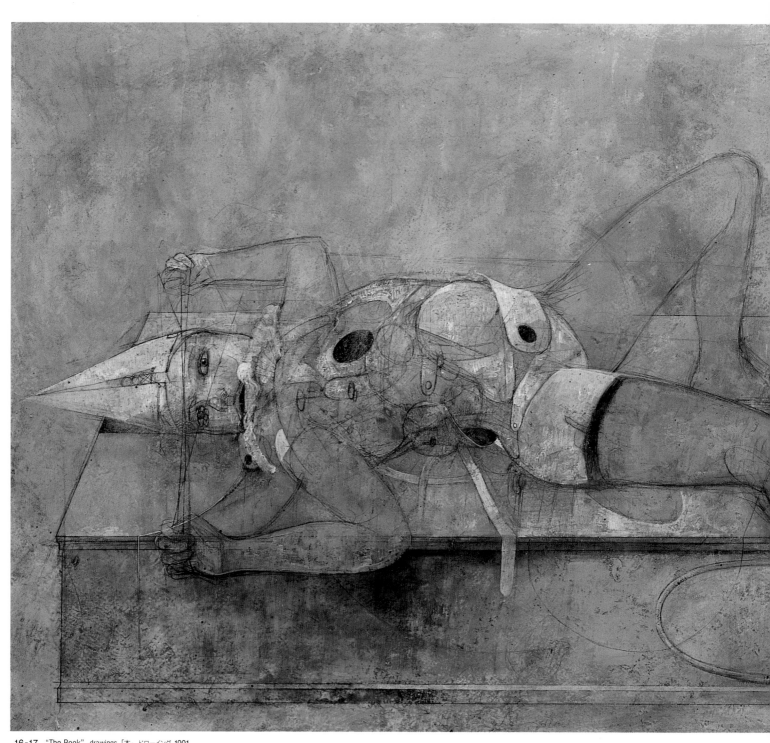

16-17 "The Book" drawings 「本」ドローイング 1991

18 Theater poster 劇場ポスター 1989

20 Film festival poster 映画祭のポスター 1991

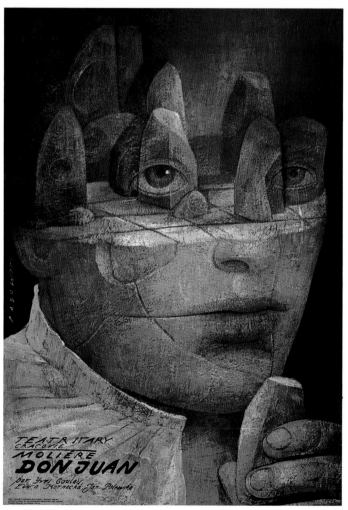

19 Theater poster 劇場ポスター 1990

TEATR WSPÓŁCZESNY WROCŁAW POLAND

ISAAC BASHEVIS SINGER   THE MAGICIAN OF LUBLIN

21 Theater poster 劇場ポスター 1987

22 "The Sensual Winter of Nineteen Eighty-nine" painting 「1989年の官能な冬」ペインティング 1989

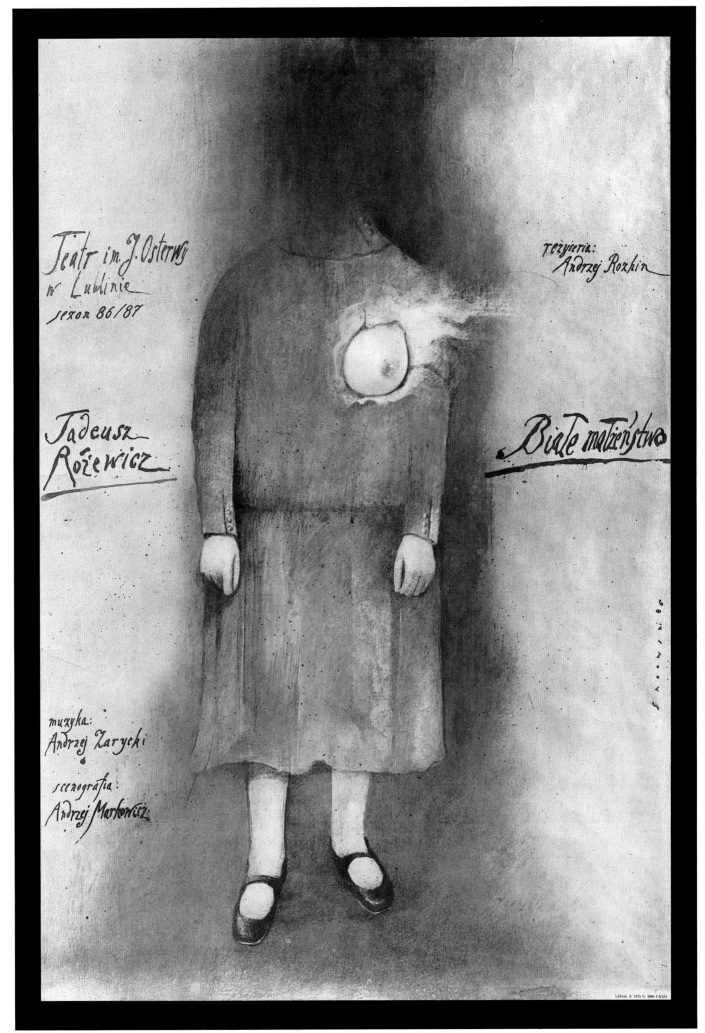

Franz Kafka Proceß

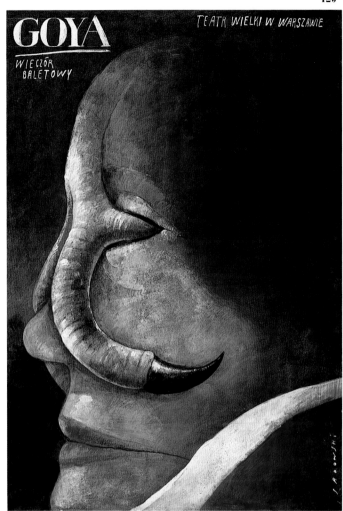

26 Theater poster 劇場ポスター 1983

25 Theater poster 劇場ポスター 1984

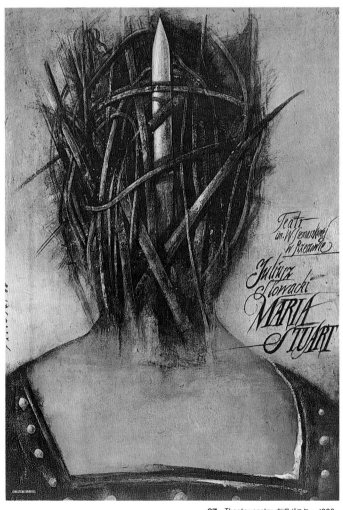

27 Theater poster 劇場ポスター 1986

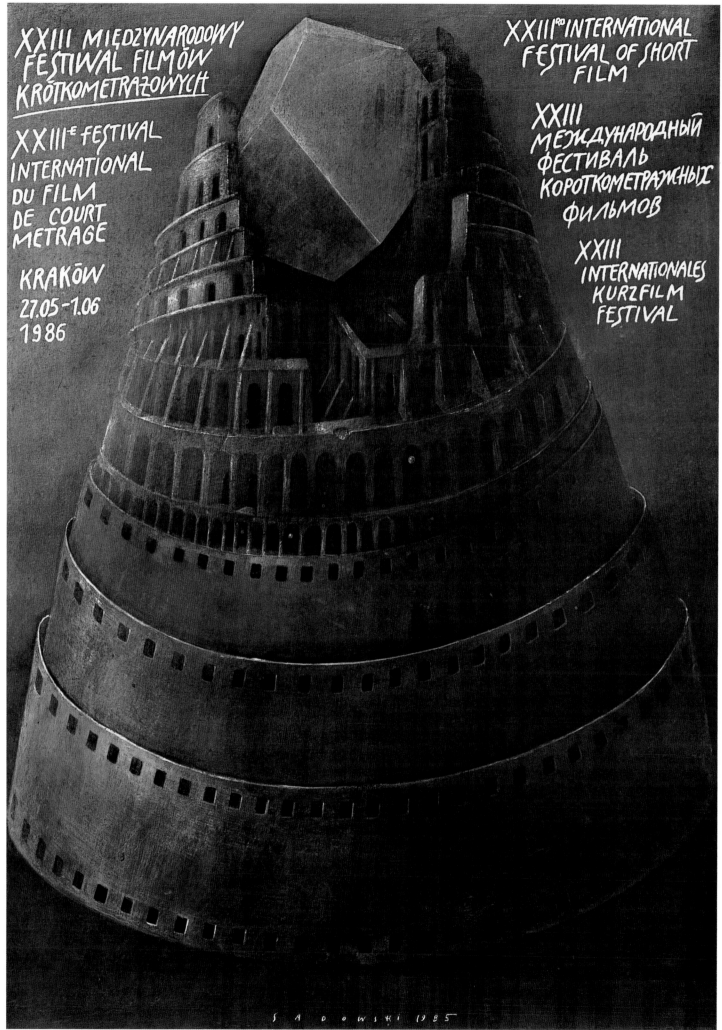

HARUO TAKINO 滝野晴夫

Ikko Tanaka 田中一光

The first time I met Haruo Takino was in the autumn of 1969 at the awards ceremony of the Japan Advertising Artists Club. The ceremony, conducted by the Club's director and several committee members including myself, took place with little fanfare in a small room in a Ginza hotel. At the time the Club was at its flourishing peak—and on the eve of its sudden demise.

Takino was present to receive an award of special merit, one of several given on the occasion. He accepted his prize without a word, all the time maintaining an air of arrogant defiance accented by a pair of pastel-colored sunglasses. A chill of unsettling premonition ran down my spine as I wondered if this young man standing before me was here for no other reason but to sabotage the Club and all it stood for. Indeed, he seemed to me to be the embodiment of the tumultuous wave of criticism that was sweeping through Japan at that time—the height of student unrest amid growing national prosperity.

Takino's award-winning work was a provocative piece showing a middle-aged man with weathered skin set in juxtaposition to his own plaster-cast model. It was a strange, beguiling work, coolly detached and lacking all human warmth. It had an inner power so forceful that I trembled to think that it might utterly destroy the Club and our insouciant view of graphic design.

Paradoxically, however, I found myself strongly attracted to Takino's weirdly distorted view. In his works I sensed the soul-searching poetry unique to those times. And so, almost in spite of myself I began to seek out his visual poems to adorn my own creations. Initially I requested his assistance in illustrating the book jackets of several volumes in a series of contemporary works of literature from around the world. Then starting in 1973 we collaborated on a series of posters for the newly opened Seibu Theater. Over a dozen posters were created, on themes ranging from Chekhov's *The Cherry Orchard* to Kobo Abe's *The Kidnaper*.

When working with Takino, one must meet certain conditions. Above all, as art director I must give him a clear image of precisely what I want. With Takino it is never enough just to suggest that he proceed as he judges to be best. With most illustrators, giving detailed instructions of this sort hurts their artistic pride and is thus generally avoided; even more so if one hands over bagfuls of material to get one's point across. But in Takino's case, his talents actually shine brightest when he is presented with a restricting framework in which to work. In this sense he is like a veteran actor who gives his best performance when his stage is perfectly set. His finished product, too, might be compared to a tower that rises majestically on the collective strength of pillars each set in place according to a clearly defined building code.

As an art style, superrealism is a slow and painstaking process. It leaves no room for errors, no room for retakes. Every brush stroke must be added individually on the long path to completion. It is on this solitary road that Takino's visual poems are born. They are poems of noble birth...poems in a league far above the speed-driven improvisations so rampant in the art world today.

滝野晴夫と初めて会ったのは(この事は前にも書いたことがあるが)隆盛をきわめていた日宣美が、突然解散する、崩壊寸前の授賞式であった。

学園紛争の真っ只中の、1969年秋のことである。この日は東銀座ホテルの小さな部屋の中で、事務局長と私たち数人の委員の手でひそやかに行なわれた。

滝野は特選作受賞者の一人として、私の前に現われた。水色のサングラスをかけたまま、彼は終始、居直ったような表情で無言で賞状を受け取った。私はもしかすると、彼がわれわれの日宣美を狙撃するために、この場に現われたのではないかというような危機感に襲われた。滝野は、その時代の思想や、感性を持った批判勢力の典型として私の目に映ったのである。

滝野の受賞作は、老いた皮膚を克明に描いた中年男性と、その石膏型を対比的に並べた、不思議な情緒をもった作品であった。高度成長期の、のんきなデザインを考えていた日宣美は、こうした冷徹な感覚によって抹殺されてしまうのではないかと思った。

しかし、私はどこか奇妙なひずみをもった滝野の感性に強く引かれるものがあった。その時代だけがもっている濃厚な詩を彼の作品に感じたからである。私は彼の詩を懸命に追うことになった。現代世界文学選書シリーズの中から、アイリス・マードックの「赤と緑」や、ジョン・ファウルズの「魔術師」などのブック・ジャケットのイラストレーションを依頼し、73年になると、せきを切ったような勢いで渋谷に出来た西武劇場のための演劇ポスターの共作が始まった。

チェーホフの「桜の園」、アンソニー・シェーファーの「スルース」、ピーター・シェーファーの「エクウス」、安部公房の「人さらい」など、十数点のポスターがある。

滝野と合作するにはいくつかの条件が要る。当然のことながら、アートディレクターが、明確なイメージをもっていなければならない。彼の場合「まあ、その辺を適当に宜しく」とはゆかないのだ。通常、アーティストを気負ったイラストレーターなら、プライドを傷つけられるような指示や、図像を具体的に伝えなくてはならない。また、その為にはかなりの量の資料を要求される。多い時は、手さげ袋二つぐらいは届けなくてはならない。

滝野芸術はそうしたがんじがらめな束縛の中で鮮やかに発酵する。完全に整えられた舞台装置の中に追い込まれた、一人の役者の名技のように、また、いくつかの制約を一本一本の柱として建った見事な楼閣のように、人々を驚かせる才気と技能を持っている。

こんをつめても、一日にそれほどはかどらないスーパーリアリズムの画法では、途中での失敗や、描き損じは許されない。完成までの長い道のりを一筆、一筆塗り込んでゆかなくてはならない。滝野の詩は、そうした孤独な密室の作業の中で生まれおちる。

そこからは、それまでのあらゆる資料が払いおとされ、最近流行しているような、から勢いの即興では近づくことの出来ない、ある種の気高いものを放っているように思うのである。

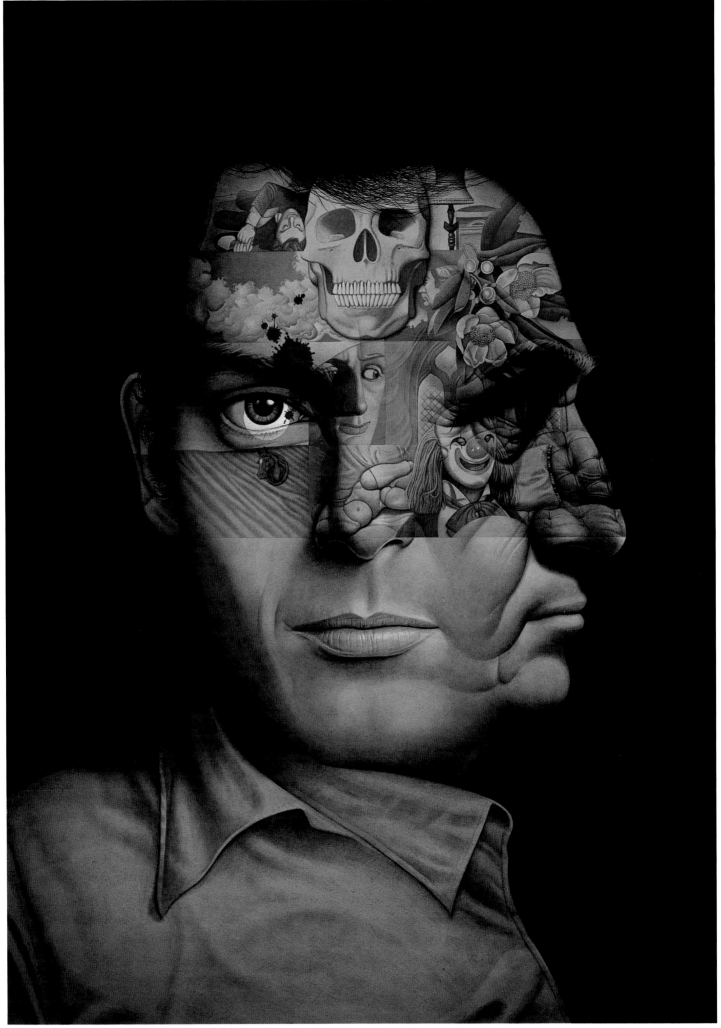

1 Illustration for theater poster AD:Ikko Tanaka 演劇ポスターのイラストレーション AD:田中一光 1973

2　Magazine illustration　AD：Ikko Tanaka　演劇ポスターのイラストレーション　AD：田中一光 1975

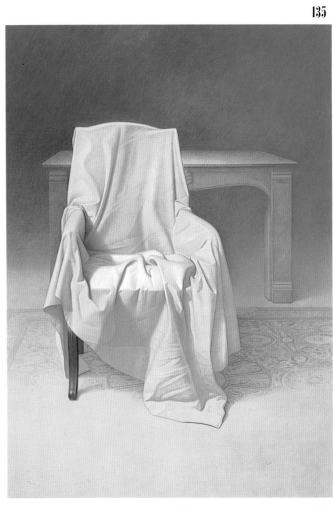

3 Illustration for theater poster AD：Ikko Tanaka 演劇ポスターのイラストレーション　AD：田中一光　1988

4 Magazine illustration 雑誌イラストレーション　1978

5 Illustration prototype for art school poster 美術学校ポスターのイラストレーション試作 1981

6　Illustration for theater poster　AD：Ikko Tanaka　演劇ポスターのイラストレーション　AD：田中一光 1977

7 Illustration for movie poster AD:Eiko Ishioka 映画ポスターのイラストレーション AD:石岡瑛子 1980

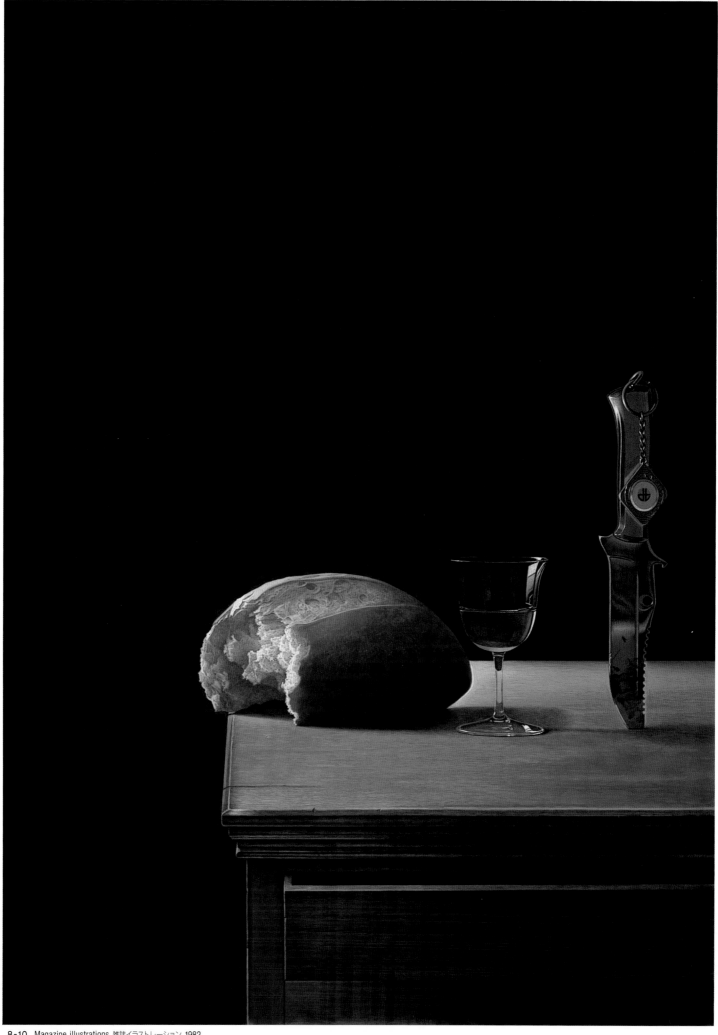

9

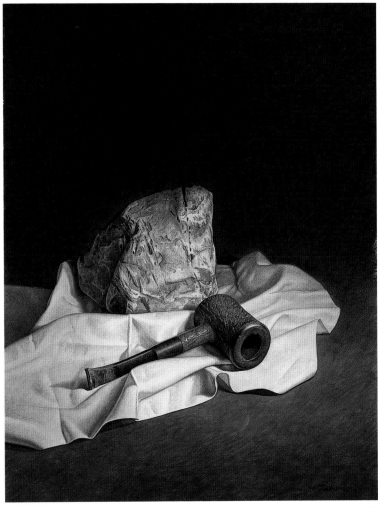

10

11　Illustration for theater poster　AD：Ikko Tanaka　演劇ポスターのイラストレーション　AD：田中一光 1987

13 Calendar illustration　AD：Ikko Tanaka　カレンダーのイラストレーション　AD：田中一光 **1978**

14 Magazine illustration　AD：Shin Matsunaga　雑誌イラストレーション　AD：松永真 **1979**

15-16　Calendar illustrations　AD:Ikko Tanaka　カレンダーのイラストレーション　AD·田中一光 1978

17

17-18 Magazine illustrations AD：Shin Matsunaga 雑誌イラストレーション AD：松永真 1982

19 Illustration for movie poster 映画ポスターのイラストレーション 1980

20　Illustration for commercial poster promoting transceivers　AD：Kaoru Kasai　トランシーバーのポスターのイラストレーション　AD：葛西薫　1979

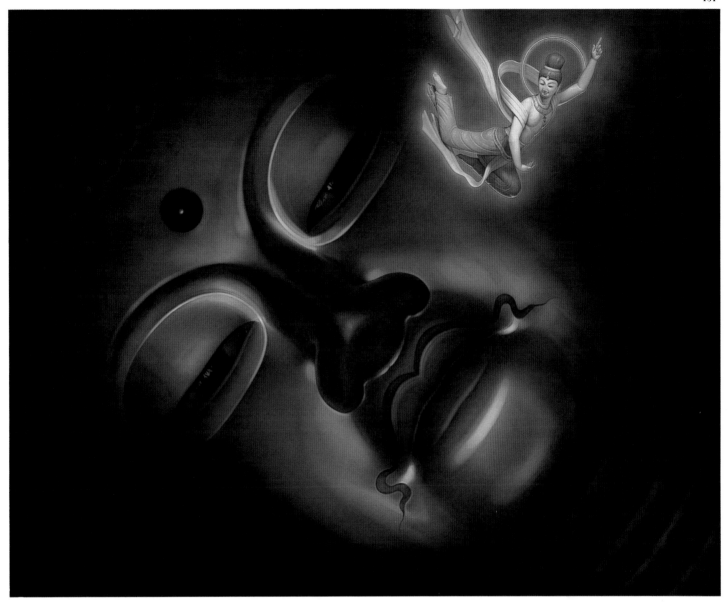

21-22　Posters promoting funerary depository　納骨堂のポスターのイラストレーション　1988

23　Illustration for theater poster　AD：Ikko Tanaka　演劇ポスターのイラストレーション　AD：田中一光 1974

24 Illustration for poster promoting poster shop AD：Ikko Tanaka ポスターショップのポスターのイラストレーション AD：田中一光 1974

25 Illustration for art museum poster AD：Ikko Tanaka 美術館ポスターのイラストレーション AD：田中一光 1975

26　Illustration for movie poster　映画ポスターのイラストレーション　1983

27　Illustration for horseracing poster　競馬ポスターのイラストレーション　1986

28　Illustration for horseracing poster　AD：Kazuya Igarashi　競馬ポスターのイラストレーション　AD：五十嵐一也　1989

29 Illustration for poster promoting fashion complex ファッションビルのポスターイラストレーション 1986

30　Illustration for poster promoting leisure resort　リゾート地ポスターのイラストレーション　1990

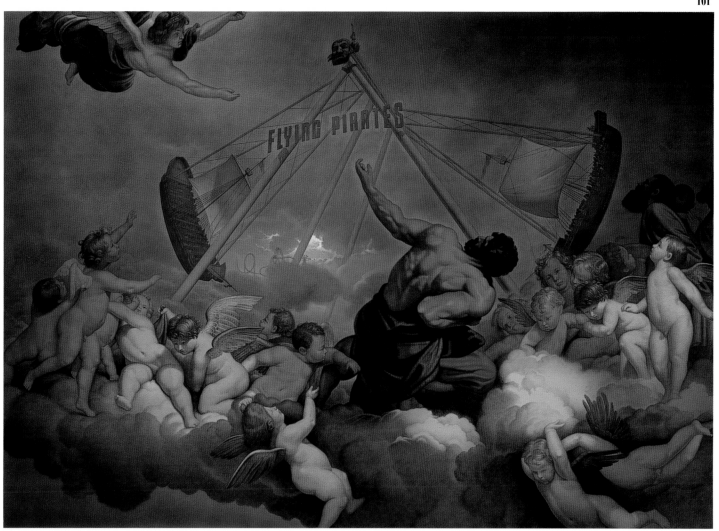

31　Illustration for amusement park poster　AD：Takuya Onuki　遊園地ポスターのイラストレーション　AD：大貫卓也 1987

32 Illustration for amusement park poster AD:Takuya Onuki 遊園地ポスターのイラストレーション AD:大貫卓也 1985

33 Illustration for movie poster AD：Eiko Ishioka 映画ポスターのイラストレーション AD：石岡瑛子 1984

ARTISTS' PROFILES
作家略歴

MILTON GLASER
ミルトン・グレーサー

U.S.A.

1929 Born in New York City.

1943-46 Educated at High School of Music and Art, N.Y.

1948-51 Attended Cooper Union Art School.

1952-53 Studied at Academy of Fine Arts in Bologna on Fulbright Scholarship.

1954-74 Co-founder (and president) of Push Pin Studios, N.Y., with Reynold Ruffins, Seymour Chwast and Edward Sorel.

1968-76 Founder, president and design director (with Clay Felker) of New York Magazine.

1974-date President of Milton Glaser, Inc., N.Y.

1983-date Founder (with Walter Bernard) of WBMG, a publication design firm, N.Y.

Mr. Glaser's work encompasses a wide range of design disciplines, e.g.: exhibition, architectural and interior design; corporate identity programs for clients in the fields of music, literature and entertainment; graphic design of restaurants; food product packaging. Recent endeavors of note include: design director for redesign of Grand Union supermarket chain; participation in design of a pavilion on "graphics in the city" for 1988 Triennale de Milano's International Exhibition; theming, signage and graphic program for restoration of Rockefeller Center's Rainbow Room. For the World Health Organization, he designed an international AIDS symbol and poster and organized an international poster event promoting public awareness of W.H.O.'s Special Program on AIDS. Mr. Glaser also holds the following positions: lecturer and board member of the School of Visual Arts, N.Y. (since 1961); board member of Cooper Union; president of the International Design Conference in Aspen; member and former vice-president of AIGA.

アメリカ

1929 ニューヨーク生まれ

1943-46 ニューヨーク音楽美術高校で学ぶ

1948-51 クーパーユニオンアートスクールに通う

1952-53 フルブライト奨学金でボローニャのアカデミー・オブ・ファイン・アーツで学ぶ

1954-74 レイノルド・ラフィンズ、シーモア・クワスト、エドワード・ソレルと共にニューヨークでブッシュピンスタジオを設立

1968-76 クレイ・フェルカーと共に「ニューヨークマガジン」を創刊。会長兼デザインディレクターをつとめる

1974- ミルトン・グレーサー・インクを設立、社長をつとめる

1983- ウォルター・バーナードと共に出版デザイン会社WBMGを設立

── グレーサーの制作はデザインの広い分野にわたっている。例えば、展覧会、建築、インテリアデザイン、音楽文芸関係のクライアントのCIプログラム、レストランのグラフィックデザイン、食品のパッケージ。
最近の主な仕事としては、グランドユニオンスーパーマーケットチェーンのデザインディレクターとしてデザインの見直し、1988年ミラノトリエンナーレ国際展のパビリオンデザインへの参加、ロックフェラーセンターレインボールーム改修のコンセプト、サイン、グラフィックプログラムに取り組んだ。

WHO世界保健機構のため、エイズの国際シンボルとポスターを制作、エイズ特別プログラムのための国際ポスターイベントを組織し、市民の自覚を促した。

ROBERTO RAMPINELLI
ロベルト・ランピネーリ

ITALY

1948 Born in Bergamo.

── Attended Scuola Superiore d'Arte del Castello in Mílan.

1980-83 Pursued International Courses at Istituto d'Arte in Urbino, studying chalcography with Renato Bruscaglia and lithography with Carlo Ceci.

1981-date Instructor of etching at Scuola d'Arte del Castello Sforzesco in Milan.

Mr. Rampinelli has worked actively both in book illustration and the publication of original graphic art portfolios (etchings and lithographs). In particular, since 1986 he has revived interest in etching techniques previously obsolete. Since 1983 he has participated in numerous individual and group exhibitions not only throughout Italy but in key locations in Europe.

イタリア

1948 ベルガモ生まれ

── ミラノのスクオラ・スペリオーレ・ダルテ・デル・カステッロに通う

1980-83 ウラビーノのイスティトゥート・ダルテで、レナト・ブルスカッリアと共に銅版画を、カルロ・チェーチと共にリトグラフィーを学ぶ

1981- ミラノのスクオラ・ダルテ・デル・カステッロ・スフォルツァでエッチングを教える

── ランピネーリは本のイラストレーション、エッチングやリトグラフの作品集を精力的に制作してきた。特に、1986年以降、以前にすたれたエッチングの技術への興味が再びわいた。1983年以来イタリアのみならずヨーロッパの主要都市で多数の個展やグループ展に出品。

DUGALD STERMER
ドゥガルド・スターマー

SHIN MATSUNAGA
松永 真

WIKTOR SADOWSKI
ヴィクトル・サドフスキ

U.S.A.
—— Born in California.
—— Graduated from UCLA with a BA in both Art and English Literature. Then worked as Design Director for studios in Los Angeles and Houston.
1964-70 Served as Art Director for *Ramparts* magazine. Thereafter went freelance first as a magazine designer, more recently as an illustrator.
1986 One-man retrospective exhibit held at the California Academy of Sciences.

Mr. Stermer's lengthy roster of clients includes the 1984 Olympic Games (design of official medals), Levi's, the San Diego Zoo, Nike, *Time* (covers), *Esquire, The New York Times, The Washington Post* and Pantheon Books, among many others. He has written extensively for *Communication Arts* magazine and is the author of two books. During his career he has won Gold and Silver Medals from the New York ADC.

アメリカ
—— カリフォルニア生まれ
—— UCLAを卒業し、美術、英文学の学士号を取得後、ロサンゼルスとヒューストンのスタジオでデザインディレクターとして仕事をする
1964-70 『ランパーツ』誌のアートディレクターを務めたのち独立し、初めは雑誌デザイナーに、また、その後にはイラストレーターになる
1986 カリフォルニア・アカデミー・オブ・サイエンスで回顧展を開催

—— スターマーの数多くあるクライアントの中でも主なものは、1984年オリンピック（公式メダルデザイン）、リーバイス、サンディエゴ動物園、ナイキ、「タイム」（表紙）、「エスクァイア」、「ニューヨーク・タイムス」、「ワシントン・ポスト」、パンテオン・ブックスなど。「コミュニケーション・アーツ」誌に度々寄稿し、著書も2冊ある。ニューヨークADCより金メダル、銀メダルを数回受賞。

JAPAN
1940 Born in Tokyo.
1964 Graduated from Tokyo National University of Fine Arts and Music with a degree in Design. Took up employment in the Advertising Department of Shiseido.
1967 Special award at Japan Advertising Artists Club exhibition.
1969 Tokyo ADC Award (also 1970, 1971, 1972, 1973, 1978).
1971 Opened his own design studio.
1985 Grand Prize at Japan Package Design 1985.
1986 Selected for inclusion in "20 Best Japanese Posters" at UNESCO exhibition of outstanding arts from around the world, in Paris.
1987 32nd Mainichi Design Award.
1988 Gold Medal and "Professor Józef Mroszczak Commemorative Medal" at 12th International Poster Biennale in Warsaw; Bronze Medal in Cultural Division at 2nd World Poster Triennale in Toyama. Held one-man exhibitions in Warsaw and Yugoslavia.
1989 30th Clio Award. Participated in international poster exhibition commemorating 200th anniversary of the French Revolution, in Paris. Held one-man show in New York.
1990 Included in exhibition of contemporary Japanese posters from the collection of the NY Museum of Modern Art, in New York. Award at 12th International Poster Biennale in Warsaw. Held one-man show in Puerto Rico.
1991 Education Minister's Art Encouragement Prize for Newcomers.

1940 東京生まれ
1964 東京芸術大学美術学部デザイン科卒業
　　　資生堂宣伝部入社
1967 日宣美展特選受賞
1969、70、71、72、73、78　東京ADC賞受賞
1971 松永真デザイン事務所設立
1985 日本のパッケージデザイン1985大賞受賞
1986 ユネスコ世界優秀芸術展・日本のベストポスター20（パリ）
1987 第32回毎日デザイン賞受賞
1988 第12回ワルシャワ国際ポスタービエンナーレ金賞、ヨゼフ・ムロシチャック教授記念賞受賞（ワルシャワ）
　　　松永真のグラフィックデザイン展（ワルシャワ）
　　　松永真のグラフィックデザイン展（ユーゴスラビア）
　　　第2回世界ポスタートリエンナーレトヤマ文化部門銅賞受賞
1989 フランス革命200周年記念国際ポスター展（パリ）
　　　松永真のグラフィックデザイン展（ニューヨーク）
　　　第30回クリオ賞受賞
1990 日本の現代ポスター・ニューヨーク近代美術館コレクション展（ニューヨーク）
　　　第12回ワルシャワ国際ポスタービエンナーレ受賞者展（ワルシャワ）
　　　松永真のグラフィックデザイン展（プエルトリコ）
　　　東京国立近代美術館・グラフィックデザインの今日展
1991 第41回芸術選奨文部大臣新人賞受賞

POLAND
1956 Born in Oleandry, Poland.
1981 Graduated from Academy of Fine Arts in Warsaw.
1984 Gold Medal, International Poster Biennale, Warsaw. Best of the Year Award, Warsaw (also 1985).
1987 Gold and Bronze Medals, International Theatre Poster Competition, West Germany. Grand Prize and two awards, International Poster Exhibit, Paris.
1988-89 Resided in New York, collaborating with galleries and publishing firms.
1989 Award from Society of Newspaper Design, U.S.A. (also 1990).
1990 Best of the Year Award, Essen. Award from International Association of Business Communicators. Silver Quill from IABC, U.S.A. Three awards at Art Directors Club 69th Annual Exhibition, U.S.A.

Mr. Sadowski is active in poster design, book illustration, painting and drawing. He has collaborated with numerous galleries, theaters and publishing firms in Poland, Germany, France, Switzerland and the U.S. Among his prominent clients have been The New York Times, Bantam Doubleday, New York Magazine, Geoffrey Beene, Penguin, Random House, etc.

ポーランド
1956 ポーランドのオレアンドリー生まれ
1981 ワルシャワアカデミー・オブ・ファイン・アーツ卒業
1984 ワルシャワ国際ポスタービエンナーレ金賞受賞
　　　ワルシャワベスト・オブ・ザ・イヤー賞受賞（1985年も同様）
1987 ドイツ国際映画ポスターコンペティション金賞、銅賞受賞
　　　パリ国際ポスター展グランプリ他、2つの賞を受賞
1988-89 ニューヨークに住み、ギャラリー、広告会社と協力関係をもつ
1989 アメリカニュースペーパーデザイン協会賞受賞（1990年も同様）
1990 第69回ADC展（アメリカ）にて3つの賞を受賞
　　　エッセンベスト・オブ・ザ・イヤー賞
　　　国際ビジネスコミュニケーターズ協会賞
　　　アメリカIABCよりシルバークイル賞

—— サドフスキはポスターデザイン、イラストレーション、ペインティングやドローイングを精力的に制作。ポーランド、ドイツ、フランス、スイス、アメリカの多くのギャラリー、劇場、広告会社と共に仕事をする。主なクライアントは、ニューヨークタイムス、バンタムダブルデー、ニューヨークマガジン、ジェフリービーン、ペンギン、ランダムハウスなど。

HARUO TAKINO
滝野晴夫

JAPAN

1944 Born in Tokyo.
1966 Graduated from Asagaya Art Academy. After working at Fukui Design Office and Asatsu Inc., went freelance in 1970.
1968 Selected for special recognition by Japan Advertising Artists Club (also 1969).
1970 ADC Award (also 1971, 1976, 1978).
1977 Gold Prize at Japan Graphic Design Show.

1944 東京生まれ
1966 阿佐ヶ谷美術学園卒業
　　　福井デザイン事務所、旭通信社を経て1970年フリーになる
1968-69 日宣美特選
1970、71、76、78 東京ADC賞受賞
1977 日本グラフィックデザイン展金賞受賞

CONTRIBUTORS' PROFILES
評論執筆者紹介

JAMES McMULLAN
Illustrator, designer, author. Principal artist of Lincoln Center Theater. Creator of High Focus Drawing Program at The School of Visual Arts, New York. President of James McMullan Inc.

SHUNSUKE KIJIMA
Art critic. Professor at Kyoritsu Women's University.

STEVEN HELLER
Senior art director of the New York Times.

MAMORU YONEKURA
Art critic. Contributing editor of Asahi Shimbun (Newspaper). Lecturer at Women's College of Fine Arts.

NOBORU MATSUURA
Graphic artist and specialist in poster history. Member of JAGDA and Japanese Society for Science of Design. Assistant Professor at Kanazawa University.

IKKO TANAKA
Graphic designer. Member of AGI. Director of JAGDA. Member of Tokyo ADC Committee.

YUSAKU KAMEKURA
Graphic designer. Member of AGI. President of JAGDA and Japan Design Committee. Editor of *CREATION*.

ジェームズ・マクマラン
イラストレーター、デザイナー、作家
リンカーンセンター劇場芸術主任、スクールオブビジュアルアーツ
ハイフォーカスドローイングプログラムクリエイター、ジェームズ・マクマラン・インク社長

木島俊介
美術評論家
共立女子大学教授

スティーブン・ヘラー
アート・ディレクター
ニューヨークタイムズシニアアートディレクター

米倉　守
美術評論家
朝日新聞客員、女子美術大学講師

松浦　昇
グラフィック・アーティスト、ポスター史研究家
JAGDA会員、日本デザイン学会会員、金沢大学助教授

田中一光
グラフィック・デザイナー
AGI会員、JAGDA理事、東京ADC委員

亀倉雄策
グラフィック・デザイナー
AGI会員、JAGDA会長、日本デザインコミッティー理事長、
本誌編集長

掲載資料のご提供を感謝致します

イタリアフォルニ画廊
鹿島建設株式会社